UNCOILING MY CORKSCREW

MARVIN WILLIAMS

ISBN: 978-0-57870-950-5

UNCOILING MY CORKSCREW

MARVIN WILLIAMS

CONTENTS

INTRODUCTION

*"Every valley shall be exalted, and every mountain
and hill shall be made low: and the crooked shall be
made straight, and the rough places plain."*

-Isaiah 40:4

I believe in the power of writing that comes from the heart. It has a magical thrill, yet its effect is undeniably real! As I write this page, sitting by a sparkling fireplace, I can't but soak in this treasurable moment.

While writing this book, there were times I couldn't breathe, and my lungs felt like a bunch of tightened knots. Strong men don't cry, some say, but I felt washed as the warm tears flowed down my face. Can you relate? Writing this book has been nothing less than a healing experience for me. Sometimes I screamed. Other times, I laughed, and many times I smiled as my whole being felt uncoiled from its screw!

There were moments when my mind played flashbacks and memories that lurked with me alone, behind the veil of my pain. I became free and alive as I began to uncoil. I'm writing to bring you to the place where your heart can be changed, and your mind can be free! Indeed, right here in your hand is a tool that can change your life forever.

I never knew I was destined to grow up like a lily among thorns, yet from the age of three, I began to grow towards that light. How could I have known that growing up without a father would be a storm for which I would need an anchor? Looking back, I now understand why I decided to wander from home at midnight to my grandmother's house at the age of three. I felt a hand was guiding me away from the severity of the storm to the solace of shores.

I was raised by some strong women who showed me what it meant to live uncoiled from the past. My mother, who was just nineteen with two kids and my grandmother, did all she could to raise her many children and grandchildren. They sheltered me from the storm and were great models when I had no one to look up to. These women seemed to know how to untangle themselves from hooks and free themselves from corks that try to pin them to the past.

Batons of grief knocked my formative years on every side with pain, failure, and pride. I grew contorted and out of control, feeling locked out from the life that I was meant to live. However, I wonder why I never tried hard enough to stop and close the chasm drilled in my soul. Likewise, I neither learned to heal the wounds of my past until the wounds began to fester.

Dealing with loss and deprivation, I got stuck in the mud, racing on the road to nowhere. Shame was never an option despite my suffering. I felt all my inner turmoil needed was a perfect screensaver that conveys success and serenity. Life, for me, was more like a stage, and I strived tediously to be a top performer. Lies became my placebo, offering temporal relief without a cure.

I fought many battles alone, got wounded in the process, and many times I had no healer, but few crutches with which I moved on with life or fought hard against my adversaries. Soon, I had to deal with pain and doubts in my life. And today, I write to help you find and fix curled points in your past that were outcomes of the loss and pain you've fought so hard and too long.

Tag along, and you'll pick gems from the hills of honesty, where you'll come face to face with your life as I came with mine, eventually. You'll find that seeking help means you're strong and not weak. It takes a real man or woman with guts to face the things they've been through. To heal from the wreckage of the past, you must be willing to be transparent with someone.

FACE TO FACE WITH MY COILS

"If something is crooked, you cannot say it is straight.
And if something is missing, you cannot say it
is there."

-Ecclesiastes 1:15

DEALING WITH THE CRAFTINESS OF LIES

"Anything is better than lie and deceit!"

-Leo Tolstoy

Truth felt like my enemy, and reality was never my friend. I grew like a tender plant, crushed in the pot of disappointment, and lack that I experienced in my life. I thought I had it all until I saw a better life, far removed from the one I always knew. Soon, unmet desires trimmed off my pride, and I could only remain as unaffected and unmoved as water in a fired kettle. But will you blame me—a rod in the furnace, beaten to shapes it never designed. Yet, my rod was coiled, did I ask for a corkscrew?

Then lies became my friends. Like flies, they flocked my mess. I never chased any of them, for they were friends with lots of benefits. I had so much shame that I needed to seal off. It didn't matter if I couldn't fix the issues buried under the cloak of deceit. All I wanted was to look better. If lies would help, then it didn't matter who gets screwed as long as I look good. Unfortunately, I became a victim of my false reality. I began to lie to myself. Then, I realized that I screwed no one except myself.

Even as I uncoiled myself from the lies that shape the life, I now call mine, I remember my deeds a kid. I kept perpetuating and justifying my embarrassments, cleaning my acts up with tidbits of lies and deceit to cover up my innocence and protect my ego.

Think about the lies that you're holding onto to relieve yourself, or probably escape the haunting comments and dire reactions of people. I've had a fair share of this human atrocity, but I can say they're not worth the least bit of lies!

PLAYING THE BLAME GAME

"Stop the blame game. Stop! Stop looking out the window and look in the mirror!"

-Eric Thomas

Your biggest victory lies on the other side of false reality; it's called truth! And who's the biggest liar? I believe it's the first person to play the blame game. Although, I always knew the *blame game* was no healer. Yet, I couldn't help it. It was my Tylenol! I was in pain! It never mattered; my coils kept increasing! I needed to be free from anger and frustration. Momma was doing her best to provide because her man had flown off the heated lines.

Even as I write this book, I remember the first thing that happened to me after my ordeals were that I blamed God and silently blamed my dad for not being there! Other times, I blamed my mother and grandmother, while always looking out for the next blame-target, I lost sight of the real enemy—the uncoiled me! I never pointed the mirror at myself, and I was too young to understand that life happens to and for everyone. It was a matter of perspective and how you perceive it to be.

And these are my questions to you: Who are you blaming for your life's circumstances? Who did you blame for where your life is today? What cunning and crafty lie do you believe about your story in life that continues to hold you hostage? When you gain the power and the tools to face your life and uncork some things that happened to you, you'll understand that all things work together for your good. It's time to stop living with a victim mentality and start *re-living* from a position of victory and dominion.

DENTED BY SELF-SABOTAGE

"We sabotage the great things in our lives because deep down, we don't feel worthy of having great things."

-Taressa Riazzi

"Don't stand in your own way!"

-Anonymous

It's interesting to know and realize how much social influences have changed us. Society, family, and friends are tremendous influences that fashion our sense of worth and confidence. Surrounded by a fiercely competitive family, I fought hard to impress. Sport was the big thing with everyone. My family earned a name in our county, and everyone felt the pressure to keep up with the game and that reputation. Always under the shadows of the discontent due to Daddy's absence, yet I fought the air to see if he'll show up anytime to say he's proud of me. I felt the need always to win. I thought my self-worth deep in a gold mine or was standing behind a finish-line, or within the ball and the basket. I fiercely competed, but rarely felt complete.

In this book, you will know that your glory is within. You don't need to bend, fight, coil, and twist to fit-in to some imagery that clouds your atmosphere from the exhaust of ceaseless expectations. Your success doesn't have to define you. You're glorious! And you make the moments, not the other way round! All you need is to keep building and working on yourself—your craft. Only make sure your craft doesn't take you to places your character can't hold!

In this book, I tell my story from the depths of my heart, because I desired to reach deep within to fix issues that won't just go away. I encourage you to do the same! For instance, my experiences with sport at several competitive levels brought me happiness, pride, and a sense of worth. But instead of managing my successes, I allowed myself to be managed and manipulated by them. I knew what I was chasing, but I never looked back to see what was chasing me. I knew what I was fighting, but never took the time to carefully assess my opponent!

I felt caught in the storm of mindsets and behaviors that bent me in shapes and forms that distorted my destiny. Like every corkscrew, I started straight, direct, and unbent; however, in the process of time, life happened, and I became coiled-up!

So, as I self-reflect and journal my way to wholeness, I am faced with the monsters that haunted me all my life. Many times, we feel we're born with a manual from the factory of life. We're filled with desires and dreams but caught between the webs of self-sabotage. Walter Scott recognized this web and moaned, *"Oh what a tangled web we weave. When first we practice to deceive."*

As we try to get out of the web, we struggle like insects in a spider's web—every unguided effort drags us deeper into the sticky webs. Soon we crave air as the cords of regrets strangle us, and a monstrous host of past mistakes catches up with us to slit the jugular and snatch off our destiny. As life fades off and slips out of our lungs, all that is left is our cry for help—that some hero will come to save and uncoil our lives.

DEALING WITH COILS OF CO-DEPENDENCY

"There are two questions a man must ask himself:
The first is, 'Where am I going?' and the second is
'Who will go with me?'
If you get these questions in the WRONG ORDER,
you are in trouble!"

-Sam Keen, author: *Fire in the Belly: On Being a Man*

I can't but feel the awe that envelopes my being as I uncoil with intense and uncomfortable self-reflection. As you read, you'll become better equipped for your journey, because I am letting you into the basement of my heart. It's a vulnerable place! I know! But I desire that you'll find release and fix issues that have coiled you out of shape.

One critical coil point is where you're crossing the line in your relationships. You're about to understand what it looks like when you cross the line from love into the co-dependency zone. My story will help you x-ray your intentions and detect ulterior motives that lurk around the love you claim and sacrifice you make. I believe that anytime you allow someone's behavior to affect you, and you are obsessed with controlling that person's behavior, you're tethering with them in the co-dependency zone.

You wonder why you deal with so many disappointments. Nobody seems to be enough—yes, no one was made to be. My life story is proof that disappointments are the first fruits of co-dependency! Do you ever wait for something and in anticipation of its arrival? You continue to get impatient and try to force the issue, bending life in your direction.

What's that package you're waiting for? Pizza, gadget, or persons, we're all waiting! How does it feel when you have absolutely no tracking device to determine their whereabouts? I've experienced anxiety waiting on something to be delivered to me. You must understand that your life's moments are precious and, sadly, fleeting! When you continue to wait on stuff that is never going to happen or people that'll ever remain a mirage, do you ask the time-question? For instance, you might be waiting on a change in your relationship. Yet, it might not be designed to be a part of your future. You might need the wisdom to let it go!

We all need to learn how to celebrate the ups and downs! That's the terrain of reality—realms without lies. I can recall developing an attachment to people innocently, which seemed like the only option at the time because I believe my love was pure. There was no balance, no idea on how to protect my heart against anything. I understood from the love my mom and grandma had shown me that love was pure and innocent!

My waiting wasn't for a package or the rain as a farmer would. My waiting wasn't for a check to pay the bills. I waited for a picture that I drew up in my mind. This book will take you into my gallery. I believe you can relate because you have yours.

My story reveals how co-dependency and waiting to be *complete* broke my heart as the bible states it so beautifully in Proverbs 13:12, *"hope deferred makes the heart sick, but a longing fulfilled is a tree of life. (NIV)"*

So, get ready to interrogate your subconscious and dig up answers that will heal the festering wound caused by waiting too long, too hard. What are you waiting for that has coiled your heart while you wait? What have you missed out on and couldn't see because your heart became sick from co-dependency?

HOW TO USE THIS BOOK

Uncoiling Your Corkscrew is not another random book on your shelf. You have chosen this book because you crave an experience. You desire a change in your life. To get the best from my inspiring stories of victory, you'll have to first, be transparent. Allow the words on these pages to be the mirror on which you'll find yourself! Please read about my life with yours in mind!

Don't be afraid to be vulnerable. Read slowly and take notes: Scribble in the margins, underline, mark-up, and draw connections as you brood over this content.

Finally, expect moments when you'll have to forgive yourself over and again as you unlock depths of hidden realities, ignored weaknesses, and covered failures that have curled over you from the past. Don't forget to act on the lessons—let wisdom mature within as you take small but bold steps. It's time to uncoil!

Are you ready?

I

THE INNOCENCE OF THE COILS

1

WHAT A BEAUTIFUL START

It all began on a beautiful moonless night. At the age of three, I wandered out of my mother's house late at night. I trolled the streets all alone. My grandmother's house was a stone throw from my mom's, yet it seemed like I had trekked over mountains and through forests to arrive there. Beyond a shadow of a doubt, whenever I hear this story, I believed that God led me to my destination.

"Who is it?" My grandmother inquired after a few rounds of faint knocks. Her response gave me a trickle of hope. She had heard a persistent sound at the door but couldn't quite figure out who was there. As she nervously walked toward the door, she wondered who could visit at that hour. Once she unbolted the door, she was surprised to see no one outside. Grandma continued to stare into the empty street with a furrowed brow until she felt a frail tug on her jammies.

I'm down here was the expression my desperate pull stamped into her heart. Filled with amazement, topped with sprinkles of confusing wonder, she picked me up and with a smile that professed the deepest kinds of love, kissed, and rocked me into bed. That was the last thing I could remember of that night!

I'll never know how a young man like myself got fortunate to be birthed by an understanding mother who recognized my need to stay with a loving grandmother. But I do know from that day up till this moment, that she has been such a guiding force in my life!

In truth, my grandmother set the tone for me at an early age. Growing up, I spent most of the years with her. Mom was 17 and a high school senior when she conceived me. Then two years later, she birthed my younger brother. Since I wandered to my grandmother's house at 3, I continued to live with her. While my brother stayed with my Mom, I remained with my grandmother until she moved to Georgia. My grand mom leaving meant I had to reside with my mom. For three years, my mom continued doing the best she could to raise both boys all by herself. I'm sure the inconveniences caused my mom to question life and she must have asked: *What am I going to do with two boys under the age of 4 while trying to figure out life as a 19-year-old?* Just within this period, I had to move back with my grandmother to live with her once she returned from Georgia on a 3-year hiatus. So, I returned to my grandma's house for the third time in my life. I bet my mom was light with relief to send me back to her mother. And I was most glad to be reunited with *mama* again. Grandma was in no way, shape, or form, perfect, but she was a pro in handling difficult situations. She had eleven kids, including my mother, and she never delayed rolling out the welcome mat for me!

From my childhood, I recall my grandmother praying for me while I slept. She knelt beside her bed every single night and prayed for what seemed like hours. She'd often place her hands on my forehead to ensure I was fast asleep, and she would begin to pray, "Lord please protect him; he's special and has such a gift inside of him. Use him and keep him from harm! Let him grow up trusting and believing in you and keep him from the traps that cause little boys like him to fail. I love you, Lord, amen!" Her prayers are some of the fondest memories I have. It was divine.

On other nights when I was tired from a nightmare, her prayers caressed me into a peaceful slumber. Sometimes, she never knew I was awake while she prayed, and I never let her know that I was. I didn't want her to stop praying for me.

Often, I wondered what happened while she prayed. I never knew at that time, but it set the framework for my life! In fact, the esteemed values and vital life lessons I gleaned from the two wonderful ladies in my life groomed me more than anything. While I could have been blamed for smashing my mother's dreams and aspirations because of my early birth, my mother never made me feel that way.

Yes, it was her choice; however, it takes great effort to keep all criticisms at bay. I think mom understood that we all make mistakes and this one was hers, yet her child was no mistake! I'm grateful to God for making her a beautiful soul anchored on the pillars of strength, love, and commitment.

Over the years, I've learned that a season of mistake isn't the time to recline in negativity. Instead, we must self-reflect and put ourselves in the shoes of others. Empathizing might require that you ask, *what would I do in similar situations?* Regardless of any hardships, we must not throw in the towel! We must strive to light up the blackness of our mistakes for multitudes to pass through without tripping. I can honestly say that although life didn't look so good on paper, I didn't realize it! I was raised by two strong women who refused to allow temporary circumstances hold them back. They never let their state of affairs fashion them into a thankless shape of being. Over the forward pages of this book, you'll witness the disastrous situations that caused my life to form into almost permanent and wiggling coils.

KEY

In a bid to answer the question of empathy I earlier proposed, I questioned my upbringing. I mean, what would I have done as a teenager caught between two stools, my kids, and my life? I'm thankful to understand that I could never have held a grudge against my mom because grandma helped her with me. It was a wise decision, and I'm proud of her! I'd be proud of anyone who invited wisdom to visit the matters of the heart! If you're in the league of children who do blame parents for their seemingly inappropriate decisions, you might be missing the fact that it was the best they could have done!

TASK:

A. *Do you still judge the decision(s) your parents made for your livelihood as a child?*

B. *What subtle things trigger you to get upset, probably some things from your past? Make an inventory.*

C. *Who do you have to forgive from your past? Why? And how can you move on and be healed from it?*

2

WHEN YOU LOSE YOURSELF TO LOSS...

The day is still clear to me 36 years later! My amazing grandmother and her friend, Gloria, took my cousin and best friend, Kisha, and I to go shopping with them and grab something to eat. We stopped by at one of the places I felt was a luxury as I grew up: *Duff's All You Can Eat Buffet.*

The food was amazing, and we watched my grandmother and her close friend talk, laugh, and enjoy each other's company all day long! Kisha and I did kid things; we hid in the clothing racks, rode on the Shopping carts, played with toys for free, and just enjoyed being out of the country woods of my hometown!

After we listened to another round of women gossip, my cousin and I reeled into a gay ambiance. Effortlessly, Kisha taught me how to pop my fingers and sing a song. I watched how she did these things with confidence and pizazz—it didn't matter that I was older. She was far ahead of her time. I couldn't quite put it in those words back then, but I recognized she was a special spritely being who *could do everything!*

Soon, we arrived at the house, said our good-byes to Aunt Gloria, and matched into our house. The fabulous memories created that day occupied my thoughts until night. We were ready for bed when Kisha squirmed, *"Marvin, tell grandma I don't feel well, my neck hurts!"* *"No problem!"* I echoed as I rushed to fetch *mama.* Grandma discovered she was searing hot and possibly had a fever. She rang up Kisha's mom, who appeared a few moments later to take her home. Grandma didn't seem alarmed, and so, I had no reason to be either.

However, the phone suddenly beeped. I could only assume the conversation by my grandma's facial expressions. She explained that Kisha was rushed to the hospital to get her better! I nodded an affirmative, *"OK!"* Although something inside my seven-year-old body felt a bit queasy, I soon slumped into sleep.

In the morning, Grandma woke me for us to visit Kisha. So, we dressed up and were soon on our way to the hospital. *Kisha was not doing well.* My heart sank in my chest. With its constant nauseating smell, I always had the notion that hospitals were scary places to be, and I didn't want my friend in it! Little did I understand what was really going on with her anyway. All I knew was that we played, laughed, and engaged in diverse bustles yesterday, and she was so lively that *sickly* could have been the last word to describe her.

When we walked into the waiting room, I remember seeing worried faces. I couldn't help but sense something was going on, and it was no good! Where I quietly sat and was scared up to my jaws like a *fraidy*

Tom, I noticed several eyes welled up! What was going on? While several questions flooded my mind, my grandmother and aunt came over and said, *you should come to see Kisha, she wants to see you*! As much as I wanted to go, my legs pinned to the ground. I was too scared to lose the apparent comfort and safety of the room to step into a scary room with all these machines connected to patients. It took me a few seconds to hear this request pop out of grown-ups and took what looked like an eternity to react to it. *"NO!"* I rejected the offer, and for some reason, I began to cry!

About 30 minutes later, I discovered that my Kisha was gone! She died from meningitis. Heat coursed through my body, and I began to sweat. Later, I didn't feel or comprehend anything. I was completely numb. *This must be a joke; she can't be gone! She was just here with me!* I panicked. In the heat of the moment, I watched everyone sob uncontrollably. Then it dawned on me that she was really gone, and I couldn't do anything about it. Her mother confirmed my nightmare when she announced Kisha's death. It was the beginning of my nightmares and a host of other undesired things. I specifically fell a part, or now, a part of me died when Kisha died!

KEY:

Was my loss obvious in my case and how did it affect me? My cousin and best friend's death dealt a mighty blow!

Here is my question to you: what have you lost in life that has caused you to lose your footing? Do you realize the source of that unaddressed pain? You might have been dealing with it for long that it is beyond pain,

---

but now a trauma. How do you stop it from leaking through every part of your life?

TASK:

Find out what has happened to you and deal with it. Whatever that may be! It is time to come out of the path of denial; you've been trailing it for too long! You may have covered your shame and embarrassment up with a disguise, but it is time to put off the mask! You must recognize that whatever the case may be, it stunted your growth, and it is time to deal with what has been dealing with you!

3

GOD IN QUESTION

For all my pain and confusion, digging deep into my knowledge and inner convictions, I knew God had a stockpile of answers available. Even when it seemed I was shadowed away from clarity, I believed that God had the master key to the solutions I craved. Lost in my frenzied thoughts, I sauntered to my grandmother's house late in the evening. And as I paced around in the backyard, hopeless thoughts flood the shores of my mind: *Why I was here on earth? Did humans just exist to die?*

I savored the orange rays that penetrated through the dusk. The sky spread with black clouds giving a hunch of a heavy downpour. I felt small. It felt like I was the only one living on the planet. I was restless and relentless! I needed answers and solutions to the inner turmoil I was experiencing. I soon find myself reclining in these fatigued questions which I couldn't even imagine God's response. *So, why God? Why is Kisha dead, and how could this have happened so suddenly? I don't understand.* I sat there and thought about it all. I felt helpless and hopeless because I approached God for more understanding, yet I felt worse. Every unanswered question haunted me, and I could only hide in its rhetoric.

Nevertheless, I continued to revel in the valley of dissatisfaction. *Why did you leave me here? What am I to do now? Where do I go or turn?* These armies of complaints ravaged my soul each passing day.

Typical of most kids, I was energetic and with tons of curiosity, and I can say that this helped in the least. My long line of questions caused my grandmother to sternly caution me, *Stop asking so many questions, Marvin!* In her famous words, she passionately said, "*No one can question God, not for good or bad.*" But how does a naive boy ride through life with an overload of fear, confusion, and uncertainty?

Innocently, I began to abandon my inner pricks and find solace in silence. Like you'd expect, trauma soon walked in to give my life a cold embrace, and there was no diagnosis or therapy insight to deliver me from its firm grip. Worse, neither my poor self nor my small community understood therapies or its essence in getting out of the siege of trauma. It was seen as a stigma, and one was considered a little loony if they ever displayed weaknesses on a mental level! Well, past that period, I discovered that many like myself would likely have undergone the treatment. But the burden of being stigmatized if people ever got a whiff of their predicament outweighed the patient's need for the actual help. So, they rescind.

As you can see, every vein in me hollered for help, but I strove to maintain my cool and appear all-fine on the surface. And to add insult to injury, I was perfect in the art! I hid it all fine.

And you see, I have come to realize that if God never fixed me, nothing else in the world would! Initially, I thought I looked up to God for some help, but I was unwilling to be helped. I was not ready to let go of my depriving and destructive habits that eat me all up.

KEY:

You must be honest about who and what is troubling you. To seek help means you are strong and not weak. It takes strength and guts to face the things you've been through. And to heal from the wreckage of your past, you must be willing to be transparent with someone.

4

MY NIGHTMARES

Something certainly happened to me when my cousin passed away. Feeling abnormal became my new normal and being awkward was a new way of life! I quickly embraced the company of solitude, silence, and sadness—well, it was all I could get.

On most nights, I would wake up with alarming screams from undesired nightmares. I'd be soaked in sweat as I narrated my ordeal of an attack to my grandmother. My emotions were completely misplaced. And I often found myself trying to explain things to people that I would not have ordinarily. Each time I asked myself why I did this, I reel off the answer that several people misunderstood me, and I have got to help them gain clarity. Rarely did I know that every time I hammered in an idea, even while nobody required it, I was growing into a stooge! I constantly was a victim of other people's emotions and taken for granted.

Beyond being trapped in the boundaries of others' emotions, I became a prisoner of no escape to my internal pains. To add up, I began to feel inferior to other people who had their acts together. I could gather that the *real me* had things going for me too. This thought burned in my head and the fire of my pain escalated that I went speechless whenever I tried to articulate the gravity of my hurt.

Sometimes, when I reflected, I did not remember harboring such painful memories in my childhood, except during my dad's absence. *But now, where did it all get wrong?*

Indeed, the things that hurt us deeply are subtle and tricky. We tend to be out of touch on an emotional level each time we experience a hurt or trauma. This period is delicate: with the ultimate option of going overboard with extreme emotions of numbness or freeze out of our feelings. I have found myself on this path, and what a joy it is to share this with you! Relating to my testimony, you will witness the oceans of weirdness, weakness, and tight*ness* that my life scaled before reaching the shores of victories.

THINK ABOUT THIS!

1. *What can you release from your past to live the heights of your true humanity?*

2. *What do you think is the bane of your struggle in this present time? Can you trace it to your past life?*

II
THE COILS BEGIN TO TAKE FORM

5
THE CRAFTINESS OF LIES

Family is everything. But I didn't find my way around every member of my family, especially my dad. He left my mom and grandma to cater for our family. And mama did a good job lavishing her love and care. I thought everything was alright, and any child of my age would have thought that, too. Until you start going to school every day, and you're startled by the clothes, rides, and class projects of *Caucasian kids* who had blue blood streaming in them. My first thought. Then, you can't help but notice the difference in your belongings and that of your friends.'

Initially, I was not moved in the slightest way about people's possessions or what I lacked. But something changed along the line. I experienced a watershed moment that made me notice these things. It was an awakening to the fact that we were okay financially, but only to the extent of scraping daily bread and basic needs. In another word, we were merely *comfortable*.

I can recall how excited I was to work on a science project in grade six. I threw myself at researching, talking, writing, and scribbling my ideas on what I'd create. Eventually, as I read one of the classroom books, I got lighted on my imminent science project. I wanted to create city lights with small telegram poles while installing Christmas lights on the pole to explain how electricity worked. *Fabulous, right?* It was the only picture I set my heart on.

However, I met with a hindrance on my way that got my dreams going to the dogs. There was just a single issue that watered down my trimmed and cut out plans: *Who would supply the equipment I needed to work with?* None of my kit and kin could afford power supply nor extras! Secretly, I was crushed for a day or two, but I internalized my brokenness. With the rubble of nerves left in me, I thought of a new idea of using old toys around the house. That would cost just a few bucks, I thought.

I started by using an old *Remote-Control Car* and took out its motor and wires. Next, I installed a propeller on the motor. This was my humble beginning in the construction of a cardboard helicopter. I rigorously studied every hypothesis, background research materials, procedure, and conclusion paperwork that I could lay hold on!

Yet, one ugly head reared up again. I needed a poster board to complete my project, but I was scared to ask. I feared being rejected, one more time. I pictured the scenario where mom will meet me with that voice and say, *"NO,"* or *"We don't have that kind of money!"* Needless to say, I waited to ask anyway. I'd rather deny myself than make *Mama* and mom feel bad for lacking the provision!

Time raced along, and I continued to nurture my dream of winning first place. Well, after a thorough thought of never getting it anywhere else, I mustered the courage to ask for the much-needed cardboard. Of course, I wasn't surprised when I didn't get the monster tri-folding poster board that I coveted! My momentum was crushed, and to my embarrassment, I had to carry my science fair project in my bookbag to school as I rode to school the next morning.

When my teacher asked if I did the project, a surge of fear and shame made me want to tell her I did not do it, but I decided to submit the *thing*. So, compared to other projects arrayed elegantly on her desk and around the classroom, I held up what should have been the next big invention but then was not worthy of a trash can! If I reserved a doubt about it being worst, my classmates kindly increased my belief that it was through their rancorous reactions. They ridiculed and picked on me until I could not put up with it any longer.

Rubbing salt in my wounds, other students who never completed their projects taunted that theirs looked better than my dilapidated helicopter! I swallowed the bitter pill of my anger and pride. Inwardly, I tried my best not to get upset with my mom and grandma.

The truth was, I blamed them. I kept on blaming them and never stopped. Soon, this blame virus spread from my parents to a wider span. I crucified others if I didn't get to show up and lied to my teacher and my friends. While I told my mates that my grandma couldn't make it on time to get my project across, I lied to my teachers that my project got broken on my way to the school. Never was I going to come clean to let them know *de Facto*, or what surrounded my unpolished project work. That would shed bad light upon my family! That's what I cut out; if a lie was going to shield my family from nasty opinions, I was in for it!

When you start to feel justified for telling a lie, something is wrong with your moral compass, and you should pause to check it! I was ignorant of this salvaging truth as a youngster. I was desperate not to look poor, so, I started lying to myself from that point on, regardless of the situation.

My teacher believed me, or so I thought, and my close friends never mentioned it again! For me, I never stopped to deal with it! Even as I write this book! I recount the most regrettable incidents of my life: I blamed God, then my mother, grandmother, and my dad, who wasn't even available to help or act as a dad should!

Indeed, life happens to every one of us, but I was too young to understand. It was easy to see other people's faults without having to point the mirror in my direction. I realized it was a matter of perspective and how we saw things. And when you gain power and needed tools to face your life and uncork some twisted happenings and beliefs, you'll understand from all perspectives that everything works together for good! You'll quit seeing yourself as a victim and start believing and behaving as the victor that you are! Then, it'll dawn on you that you're bigger than your lies!

TASK

So, my question to you is:

1. *Who are you blaming for your life circumstances?*

---

2. What cunning and crafty lie do you continually believe about your life that continues to hold you hostage?

6

HERO TO ZERO

I grew up in a competitive family where every person was an athlete. It was competitive because each one was silently expected to attain and keep up with a level of success. My mom used to go like a bomb as she raced on the track. I witnessed her playing softball and saw how effortlessly she played. Her position was either shortstop or third base, and she could field, throw, and run! I can remember watching her from the stands and tooting my horn that she was my mother!

My uncle and aunt all grew up and made names for themselves among the best athletes in the city. To compensate for our hard work and sportsmanship, my family, the *McIntyre's*, had a post in the local newspaper that read 'When you say Martin County, say *McIntyre*," on the front page of the sports section. So, to be a part of the family, you knew what was required: you had to excel in sports!

No surprise, I was involved in the youth's sport from a tender age. My uncles groomed me, and I had to practice winning! I competed in dribble, shoot, and free throw contests. I played baseball as a pitcher and shortstop; football as the quarterback and wide receiver; and basketball as the point and shooting guard. I won many ribbons from the trios, which I constantly prided in.

It hurt deeply if I lost a game. Usually, I cried, and I spent the next few days, sulking. As much as taking things personally has its bad sides, this attitude propelled me to prepare for each game immensely. And it set me apart in sports.

At a point in my 7th grade, I stepped up to the free-throw line with only a second to go. We were down by one. It was a situational free-throw called *one and one*, which means, if I made the first one, I'd get the second attempt. Swiftly, I made the first free throw that got us a tie. It was my first time undertaking such and holding the ball in a fully packed gymnasium, with all eyes on me kind of felt eerie. I dribbled and made sure I repeated every routine I practiced in my daily throws. I picked up the ball, took a deep breath, bent my knees, and let it fly!

It seemed the ball hung in midair for up to 10 slowing minutes. As the ball approached the rim, I continued to follow it with my eyes. Out and out, the crowd was silent. Amid the deafening silence, I heard the nets go swoosh! Game over. And in the next second, I heard the crowd chant my name. My teammates picked me up, and much excitement filled the gym. It was a slim chance of victory maximized at its fullest.

However, my celebration was brief. With friendly pats on the back and ecstatic cheers, I passed over hugs to look for my dad. I gave an ear to the compliments but longed to hear my dad applaud me. I felt that being the game-winner was all for nothing because the man I strove to impress the most was nowhere to be found. As we flooded the locker room to get dressed, my coach and teammates applauded me like a hero. Yet, I didn't feel a bit of the praise as dad's absence made me feel less and less unworthy of every praise rendered.

However, like a bolt from the blue, my maternal grandfather was present at the room entrance to give me a smile and a vote of confidence. He was a man of few words, but I knew that he was proud of me. It eased the pain. I discovered that some girls were waiting for me to trumpet how awesome I played, and it made me feel on top of the world! The scales of shyness fell off me, and I thought of myself like a new man. I was now *man enough*. In my head.

That game changed my life! All eyes were now on me, and it felt good for a change. The next day, I bounced into school chests out and my head high. Tons of girls flirted with me, and I could choose which one would be my girlfriend. Having all the girls' attention increased my ego. But like a cologne scent, my success soon faded off. Just as fast as I was as a hero, two days later, my world came crashing down in the same gym, playing the same game, but with a different altitude and attitude.

If I could turn time's hands and returned to ask some of my teammates, they would probably say that I played selfishly. It showed in my statistics how much I played terribly. The coach had to bench me and remarked, *"You went from a hero to a goat!"* This statement fractured my already cracked spirit. I didn't know what it meant, but from the energy with which he said it, I knew it was up to no good. I shrank in the disgrace and pain that hit me. I craved approval and validation for me to get back on my feet. I believed it'll come from me racking up several goals. But I came to the awareness that whenever you turn to anything outside of yourself to make you feel better, you are immediately out of balance.

It's the easiest thing on earth, to look up to something else to validate you. I experienced this firsthand. Although I felt so good as I gained recognition for doing something *cool*, it was also cancerous. Why is that? I became prideful as I received praise and adoration from a horde of my schoolmates. And you know it, just as the Scripture puts it Proverbs 18:12: *"Before a downfall the heart is haughty,"* I didn't realize that I was heading for my downfall!

TASK:

1. What are you allowing to validate you?

2. What are you hiding behind?

3. Who or what do you project to make yourself feel better?

4. When the glorious moments of your life fade, do you still believe you're as glorious as the moment?

5. Are you even aware that it's you who is really glorious, and it's you who make the moment?

7

JOKES ON ME

Have you ever been the butt of someone's joke? What about the entire school knowing embarrassing secrets about you, and worst, they chew on it for the longest time? All of us have had some situations that we wished had never happened. While a few people get to heal, others might rise up to do things that send off their bad deed into oblivion, and yet, many continue to tread the irritating path of their open secret. In my case, I crawled on along the hideous road in such a way that it almost got my feet crippled. What happened to me caused my head to look like an episode from *Martin Lawrence's fat head*. It was like walking around with a head that could fit on an elephant's body.

Relating to my coil of embarrassment, a story stands out to me. I was trying all too well trying to impress my friends and wanted to tell them about a sexual experience I never had. Stories about their sexual adventures made me feel less of myself. I thought I was the only oddball that didn't have sex in middle school. They pressured me, and when they asked, I put up the lie, *"Of course I did, but I won't tell you guys who because she'd get in trouble if anyone found out."*

One particular day, my *so-called* girlfriend told me she was coming over after school. As a sporty and arrogant god's-gift-to-the-girls' guy, I quickly conceded. My grandma at the time was a bus driver, and I knew her schedule like clockwork. I was usually home alone for about an hour and a half. I took the free time to snack, do my homework, and watch TV. Sometimes, I'll go outside to play with a couple of friends when I completed my tasks.

A few school friends knew that I was expecting a visitor as I told them while we strolled home. They continually asked, *"What are you going to do?"* And with the queer but well-known smile, I hit them with my egotistical response, *"Guys, you already know."*

Deep within, I was scared, but I wasn't going to let it show. I was going to glow with the come-forth scene. The guys absolutely wanted me to have a story to tell the next day. With every step closer to my house, I could feel my heart jump right of my chest as I thought about the upcoming episode. Immediately I got in, I began to get nervous and developed cold feet. Of course, I didn't want to have sex, and from the conversation I had with the young lady, that was her only aim. She wanted to jump my 12-13-year-old bones. I didn't know what to do or say, except that I was replaying the horrible scenes and porn videos prescribed to me unbeknownst to stimulate my sex drive. It was disgusting and confusing all at once.

Even when I had enough willpower, the question is what I would choose. I glanced at the wall clock and knew I had to figure it out within the final 10 minutes of waiting. *Maybe she won't come. Maybe she'll chicken out. Maybe she was lying.* I hoped those thoughts were the truth as I paced the hard-concrete floor. My anticipation grew with every tick of the clock. Instantly, I heard a thud on the front door! On the spur of the moment, I pretended that I wasn't home. In some degree of noiseless speed, I took off through the back door. I ran like a deer being pursued by a lion. However, as I maneuvered through a narrow footpath behind my house, I was met with the surprise of my life!

I noticed some guys hanging around my home, possibly to hear what was happening or to peek on *us*. Never in a million years would they figure they would see their friend run for what seemed like his life. On my hand, my friends were the rarest set I wanted to crash into as I leaped for my purity.

My girlfriend was still pounding on my door, probably confused about not getting a response. She was completely shut out away from my current escapades going on at my unfenced little backyard. One of the guys informed her that I ran into the safety of a friend's house to escape her presence. As much as I was pleased that I escaped having a sexual encounter that I really hated to happen, I had discomfited myself by my fearful flight! I could imagine what the talk would be at school the next day. The latest topic would take this form: *Marvin ran like a girl*! The next morning.

On the 20 to 25-minute walk, I tried to figure out how to evade the looming embarrassment of what should have been something admirable. *What do you do when you're trying to do the right thing but get blasted for it as if it's a plague?* I couldn't tell my grandmother what was happening because, in no way, shape, or form was I going to let her know I invited a girl to the house. So, that was off the table.

The walk to school was already rugged with humiliation. There was no way this hero would sit in school for 7 hours, exposed to a pack of wolves ready to tear him apart. So, I decided to walk a little behind. Fortunately, one dear friend of mine saw through my pains and encouraged me. He told me it was OK, but it was only a piece of cake for him to say that! I'll be the one to fight the claws of the lion, after all.

Like a switch to a light bulb, a brilliant idea lighted up my mind. I made up my mind to stay clear of the cafeteria, I decided to trip and fall purposely. I'd make sure I hit my knee as I fell. As if the universe responded to my conceived idea, I stumbled upon a drain with a steel knob attached to it. Without another thought, I fell directly on it. When my friend noticed that I fell and heard my yell, he asked me to stay down while he fetched help. Yes! That was it! As I laid on that ground alone, I thought it wasn't enough to keep me from school. Once more, I hit my knee hard on the steel so that I'd get injured.

A handful of minutes later, my friend came through with a school employee, Ms. Elaine, who knew my family. She asked, "Boy, are you hurt?" "Yes, ma'am!" I hastily replied. She didn't have to consult with the school before she called my grandmother. Ms. Elaine was a woman of discipline who didn't tolerate any kind of frivolity. And as we usually said in my town, she didn't play. I felt since I could fool her, I'll successfully fool anyone too.

The doctor confirmed my injury to be a cracked knee. I was definitely sure that it wasn't the case, but I was wise enough to keep it to myself. The recent announcement gave me a pass to stay home for a week, so I could get used to walking on crutches, and I could fare well with not being picked on all week long! Rather than being burdened with bullying, I received loads and loads of empathy and sympathy. Truly but sadly, this was my way of dealing with life for a long time. I comfortably fooled others for a justifiable cause.

The coils of lying, manipulating, and justifying had just begun to take form a deep form.

TASK:

1. From your childhood, what story of embarrassment do you keep on perpetuating or justifying?

2. What have you lied about to cover up your innocence and protect your ego?

3. What are you holding onto that you feel you can't tell people?

4. "They're all going to laugh at me" is that a phrase that still haunts you? What is it?

5. What coils can you identify in your life by reading this story?

*At this point, I'd like to inform you that your biggest victory lies on the other side of false reality, and it's called truth! -I Am Gleason

8

...BEFORE THEY SHOW UP!

Do you ever wait for something, and while you anticipate its arrival, you get impatient and try to speed it up? It could be a package. You might go online and trace the tracking number, and then try to get a better idea of where your package is. It brings you comfort to understand the holdup and the whereabouts of your package. Even if you don't receive it, you get a sense of calm because you can focus on the whereabouts of your important package with a continuous flash of knowledge.

Well, what if your package is human, and you have no tracking device at all to determine the whereabouts? Just like the case with my dad. I wanted to receive a father's love, but he was never home. I wished I could speed up the waiting process up to the time he'd fully come for me. But a man is an entirely different kind of package. I didn't possess the punch button to get him down where I was. So, I had to make do with the surpassing love I received from other relatives.

I received immense love and support from my grandmothers, grandfathers, aunts, and uncles. Even through my grand uncle JD although his slowness was distasteful, *he* showered me with love and attention. For instance, everyone got frustrated when my uncle JD would take me for a ride in his car, because it was hours before he would return, because of his slowness. He slowly drove as if he'd harm its occupant if he went fast.

For some reason, the comfort of being protected and loved came easy with him around. I saw myself running on the front lawn and have my uncle make sure that I didn't run in the road. I often had the sense of being in a dark room and feeling his eyes spotlight my steps, so I wouldn't harm myself—that was love.

Above and beyond, my grandma always catered for me with great care. Grandma cooked my favorite meals after we returned from the grocery store. She'll prepare pancakes and everything I asked, no matter when I did. She taught me what love was as I spent my life with her.

While I experienced anxiety waiting on a person I loved to show up, I had to welcome people ready to love me without delay. What are you waiting on that's yet to be delivered? Are you waiting on your relationship to change when it wasn't even designed to be a part of your future? Understand that it was ordained to bring you to where you are now. Celebrate the *ups* you had and heal from the *downs* that dragged you past pain. But most of all, let it go and ride on the wings of wisdom, healing and move on!

Back then, I innocently developed an attachment to people. It seemed like the only option for me at the time, as I believed in giving and receiving love. I knew nothing else than to love and accept people just as they were. Instead of offering a reciprocated love, people hated, hurt, and mocked me! I shuddered under the weight of imbalance and had no idea on how to break free from my desire to always love others.

I was an open love tank where every Tom, Dick, and Harry could draw from without refilling. Meanwhile, I drew the roots of my *love-dispenser* from mom and grandma's teachings that love was pure and innocent. My *Ma* and *Mama*, which I religiously called them, nurtured me to experience the beauty of complete and fulfilled love—no *filter*, no ego, and no expectation.

Who was the example of love for you? If you encountered pain from your supposed love example, are you perpetuating the same cycle? Are you waiting on love to show up again? Maybe you're waiting on a love typical of your dad, mom, sibling, or grandparents to materialize in your neighbor or associate. Or could it be that you want the pureness of unadulterated love as you remember from your past?

Not showing up translates as the opposite of love to me! I waited for him at the basketball games. I'm referring to my dad here. I waited for him to pick me up at school. I waited for him at my dinner table. I waited for him to throw the ball back to me and even imagined him talking to me. I anticipated my dad's arrival every Christmas. I pictured him and my mom living happily ever after.

Rather than play out mental activities that cloud my brain, He'd only stroll in and out. Then, the endless wait-cycle began spinning again. An old wife's story is weight broke the wagon. My story says: wait broke my heart! And the Bible reiterates in Proverbs 13:12; *"Hope deferred makes the heart sick, but longing fulfilled is a tree of life"* (NIV).

Flowing from a healed and mature heart, now, I'll say, I've learned to put myself in other's shoes and see from their standpoints. Like I mentioned in the earlier chapters, life happens for everyone. But I must determine how I look at my situation. Is it from the perspective of love that conquers all (1 Corinthians 2:9), or from the view of defeat? You have it in you to be the channel of love—to love anyone and everyone. Tune in to the station self-less love and disconnect the channel you don't want to ever show, on your preview guide.

TASK

My question to you is:

1. *What are you waiting on that has troubled your heart?*

2. *What have you missed out on and couldn't see because your heart was sick?*

9

I WANT MORE!

"...It's never enough, I want more!"

Hanging out with friends who were of a different nationality and being exposed to their lifestyle did a single thing for me. It spotlighted what we lacked in our home while taking stock of what they had. On my first visit to a Caucasian classmate's house, I noticed two beautiful cars in the driveway. They didn't have to share the front yard! As I entered their home, the large television set caught my eye. Taking a walk through the rooms, I observed that a TV set was installed in each room. It was huge!

It got to me that they weren't trying to brag in the least opportunity but showing me around was their way of making me feel comfortable. After the tour session, all I could think of was, *"we don't have any of this kind of stuff."*

On another visit to the Caucasian House, I ran into the man of the house, Dad. I immediately became uncomfortable and was forced to admit that we merely survived back in our house, and our family structure was different. It was no indictment on my family status. Not in a million years will I express dissatisfaction with my family. I preferred to protect their feelings while I crushed mine. Well, after all, *Ma* and *Mama* did their best in the way they knew how to. I endured the narrow circumstances until I recognized that life could be different.

Honestly, I had that notion but waived it off since I was uncertain of what it really was. Even though I masked on as indifferent, I was unhappy about our lifestyle. I got a new perspective about our meager apartment, which was no match to my friend's beautifully structured home that distinctly sat in its own fenced-in yard. This thought was constantly a sign of my dissatisfaction with my reality.

At a point, a friend called to come over. It was a big deal for him to obtain permission to cross tracks to come to my neighborhood and much more, he wasn't afraid to come! I talked him into canceling because I was ashamed to allow him to see where I lived. Was it the shared dirt driveway that wouldn't be an eyesore or the half-grass-half-dirt yard? There was no beauty left to savor, where I lived.

The issue of having a defective image always kept me grasping at the straws of life. It trailed my journey of false reality—when I never had anything and yet pretended to have it all! For example, when my friends from another neighborhood would ask to come over, I took them to my neighborhood friend's house because, of course, my house was in shambles. Since my friends Lloyd and Chris lived in a better Home than mine, their home was my go-to. I received all my visitors there.

Soon, I would go directly over to my friends' houses after school hours. It was a nice and cozy home, and I loved to spend time within the home as much as I loved to spend time with my friends. However, every night I spent living in their house fed me with a hunger for more comfort, more money, and more wealth.

At school, I didn't turn in the free lunch form, even though I desperately needed the food. I did so just to be perceived as a part of the prestigious upper class. Can you imagine the consequences of my thoughtless action? I struggled to get a lunch money every day. I did well to hide my acts from my mother and could only wonder what will go through her mind when the cat is let out of the bag! Probably, as she reads these lines!

The pain of trying to be something you aren't to win other's approval, while you distance yourself from people who truly know the real you, are uncalled for. It never pulled off then, nor does it now. This consistent behavior stemmed from not being comfortable with being uncomfortable, and a lack of understanding that I was parading around in my trauma suit. Cloaked in a trauma outfit, I danced around through issues to protect the image of others while my feelings are relinquished to heartbreak and ceaseless bleeding from several issues. But over the long years, I've spent countless hours, days, weeks, and years to live my truth and be the writer that I've always hoped to be. Steadily, God rescues me from the siege of untold truth, forgives me for holding silent grudges, and keeps on bringing me to the sacred place of truth.

Freedom costs a fortune. I ventured into liberty without a care for what wounds must be open or pain must be relived again. So, at the expense of hurting others' feelings, placing a black eye on my family, and possibly being ridiculed for breaking out of the norm and the cycle perpetuating itself, I reveled in the freedom that accompanied my reality. With tears streaming down my face and tremor pulsing in my heart, I resolve to walk in my freedom.

With so much serene and peace that comes with living your true self, I can dig into my gold calling of leading people who live in self-denial. I'm sent to those who lie to themselves while they try to hide their scars. I'm called to help you identify where your coils of emotional damage began to take form, to point out the behavior you exude because of your coils, and to disrupt the coils that have implanted themselves in your life. Not to stop there, but to ultimately free and change the dynamics of your family.

I suffered a great identity crisis, yet I was destined to walk in freedom. So, the damaging emotional baggage is not a part of my scripts on life's stage any longer. Every form of hiding, faking, lying, and manipulating must stop with me. Are you ready to be the next to be freed? If so, let's go deeper into uncoiling my corkscrew. I'll identify and pluck into what we dealt with or are dealing with in the next chapter!

III
THE MATURATION
OF THE COILS

10

HE'S BRAGGING ABOUT ME

To know my grandfather is to love him. Each time we visited places together, he was often well-known and with several admirers. He had a lofty stature but was a gentle and polite soul who wouldn't even harm a flea. He was of a private personality and was particularly passionate about sports. He detested seeing anyone play a game being lackadaisical or without an intense drive to win. The only time he got upset was when you didn't perform well or do your best to win. Losing is no option for my grandfather.

We drove to foreign cities together, but as we passed people in the car, I'd hear them yell, *"Hello, Mr. Sonpepper!* Or *"Hello, Pep!"* for short. Till now, I'm amazed that he picked up the name as his penname. But that wasn't my interest. My biggest interest was being in that car with him, and knowing I was his sidekick, at least that's how others addressed me because we were always together. If you asked my host of cousins, most of them would say they were his favorite. Since this is my story and my truth, we all know I was his favorite, without a haggle.

In the summer of my 8th-grade year, heading to the 9th grade, I find the story of our annual summer basketball camp quite interesting. The high school coach of my potential school brought his high school team to play against guys like us anticipating high school. It was a big annual event, and I looked forward to it.

We played, and my grandfather was there to watch the game. He figured it out that I wanted to make him proud and compete in the best way that I ever could. I was a skinny kid with little muscle mass, but I held up against stronger, taller, and older guys. I scored, played great defense, and assisted on some plays. Eventually, we won the game against the high school team. That boosted my confidence! And to butter the celebration, my grandfather told the high school coach with an air of pride, "My son is a special player, you know. Did you see what he was doing to your guys? I don't know if I want him to come to your school." He was lathering it on pretty thick, and I enjoyed every minute of it.

When we drove home, he gave me a vote of confidence I'd always live to remember. In his words, he said, "If you play hard and give your all, all the time, you will make it." Straightaway, I knew basketball was going to be my thing. I had something special, and my grandfather had confirmed that. He couldn't wait for me to play high school ball. It seemed in every sport's event we went to; he didn't fail to inform the guys that I was special. I now understand that he caused that confidence and inner drive in me that still burns to this day. And every day I tell myself, "*Thanks, dad. I won't let you down!*"

Off and Running

I started high school sooner than most kids. I approached that big high school campus in the summer two weeks before school started. I played football, and we had what all footballers hate, *two-a-days*. That means you practice twice daily, conditioning, and getting your body acclimated to the uphill climb of the football season.

Naturally, I was a basketball player, much because I didn't like to get hit. However, I played and excelled in all sports. I was a perfect athlete, and this was normal because many of my friends did the same thing.

Joining the football team, I was taken aback by the size of these guys. Also, the number of people working out for the football team seemed intimidating. Again, I came from a tiny team, and having 30 players on each team right here was amazing. Now, I looked at 100 kids spread out in the summer sun who comprise a football team. It was a great feat to aim at, but I was ready! During those periods, we trained rigorously. We ran and ran and ran some more. I witnessed guys vomit, pass out, and quit. I wasn't used to that where I grew up. At least, until this point. We were required to lift a huge weight, but I rose to the task. I excelled on the football field, but I didn't play in a club. Unless I just so happen to have the shirt stuffed into my locker.

Two-a-days was over. I made the team prideful and was on my way to my new high school like a deer in headlights. The night before school started, I couldn't sleep. I tried on my new clothes thrice and asked my brother how it looked while I beamed with excitement. All the embarrassment I endured at middle school was over. At least, that was my thinking. Tossing from one side of my bed to another, I asked my brother, "Are you asleep?" "NO," he replied. He continued, "Brother, you're going to high school." I smiled in the dark and said, "Yeah" with confidence, while silently shaking under my covers in my twin-sized bed.

This was a journey that was foreign to me. I was convinced that the lessons I garnered from sports and girls could be a flashlight in an unprecedented environment. I got off my beautiful bright yellow bus, and as soon as I stepped foot on that campus, it hit me that this was a different world, entirely. I saw grown boys with mustaches, beards, and huge muscles. Girls with make-up on, wearing tight fitting skirts to reveal their womanly body shape. I considered myself one more time: I was skinny, maybe 5'7, and 155 pounds soaking wet. High school was beyond my wildest imaginations.

Sooner than I thought, I began to take baby steps and found my footing across the four corners of the school. I stumbled on familiar faces, that I had earlier met during the training. Sports were a major pillar for me while I stayed on in school. I believed if it weren't for those reasons, I would have found a way to run home. I had no time to feel sorry for myself but set myself to achieve my dream and get in the flow.

11

A NEW WORLD

I could relate the most to the 9th-grade assembly on the first day I arrived at high school. The 9th-grade assembly was to get us acclimated with the school's rules and expectations for students. I noticed a distinctive man that had a different way of walking or limping. He was a dark man with a stone face. His speech and its undeniable impact ring in my head.

He said three things that ring true today. Firstly, he said, "Look around at the people sitting next to you. All of them won't be here four years from now when you graduate. Don't let it be you." Secondly, "If you would point out your friends, I'll predict your future," Finally, he said, "If you're not here in school for business, you have no business here." As a little kid out in the adult world to make his marks, I felt that this was harsh. But for some reason, I found the words quite impactful and eye-opening.

Today, I better understand Mr. McHardy. I understand what he said and its meaning. However, while on campus, things began spinning out of control. I was a pretty smart and unusual kid who hated school. I didn't take classroom attendance seriously, and of course, the detriment of this caused my grades to slack. I believe I went to school for sports and girls' sake! I was living the life of a rock star, although it was momentary. I recollect my teacher reiterated, "This isn't middle school, we're not going to hold your hand." So, I responded, "Ok. In that case, I'll have to do what I want."

Well, just as every action has a reaction and every cause has an effect, my bad decision drove me to failure. I began to fail miserably. I scurried along from one teacher's desk to another, trying to find out what I needed to do to continue in sports. Naturally, good grades are meant to up student's performance in my school. And my grades fostered my participation in football. With basketball season coming up, my report forthcoming report card will say a lot if I could partake or not. I knew trouble bellowed. Although I was active in football, I couldn't miss the basketball season. I did everything within my power to raise my grades. When it guaranteed no promises, I took advantage and reached into my bag of tricks that previously worked for me—that same knee I hurt in middle school. Or pretended to hurt. I took a fake dive into the football field and decided to fake an injury. I wasn't hurt, but this idea worked better. I couldn't think of letting *Pep* down by not playing basketball. So, if being hurt was the reason I couldn't play, and faking again, here I go.

Unexpectedly, the vicious cycle had started to repeat itself. I began to lie and behave fraudulently. I manipulated both my teachers and classmates and shun responsibilities; my entire life was full of lies. The coils in my corkscrew were winding very tight. I was in a mess because

I failed to realize this self-styled injury couldn't last the duration of the basketball season. And wow, look who got tricked! I had to own up. My uncle was a basketball coach at my school, and if anyone knew the truth, it was him. They'll all get to find out. So, I decided I'd face the facts and live with the embarrassment of failure of letting my grandfather down.

Matter of fact, I let myself down. It was my reward for living an undisciplined and selfish life. My world was starting to crash, and my trick source couldn't prevent the destruction that purred. Most times, we get stuck on the external behavior of a person, without understanding the inner turmoil that is merely surfaced through outer behavior. This recipe of deceit that my grandfather was unaware of, and the pressure I put on myself not to let him down, only led me to do one thing; let him down.

12

INNER SECRETS WITHOUT AN OUTER FACE

Someone said, *"What is your problem?"* The better question would have been, *"Why didn't I attend class?"* When did I learn to disobey my parents' rules? They told me I had to get good grades, play sports with my God-given talent, and excel in it. It sounded easy, but not for a kid who would sit spaced out in class and would try to control being fidgety all the time.

Also, I was now labeled with *OCD* (Obsessive Compulsive Disorder). While I ate, I constantly counted the number of years my cousin would have been alive, and then I took a walk before I swallowed. For instance, if she were eight that year, I would walk eight steps and swallow, and I must end on my right foot. This sounds both exhausting and crazy, but it was my all-day behavior. For some reason, I still struggled to forget about her. I don't believe anyone knew.

I appeared in class, stone-faced, and stared at the teacher without hearing a single word. Even worse, I didn't see them. This wasn't because I had a comprehension issue. It was more of the fact that I had internalized issues. I would try to control my agitated movement or my inability to be still. So, at the expense of my learning, I became focused on me not sticking out like a sore thumb in a class.

I'm sure my classmates would act up all rude and cruel if they knew that I dealt with that. Therefore, I found it quite convenient while I stalled at P. E. classes. I skipped classes out of the necessity to protect my inner struggle and ego. I opted to fail to protect my self-image. In no time, the pain of sweeping my weaknesses all under the rug was starting to become unbearable. But did it matter what I felt? I was bent on making it look easy and I believed I made it seem so—in my head.

13
DON'T WAKE ME UP!

Have you ever wished some unbearable parts of your life away? Or have you been burdened by the weight in your life that you hoped you could run from it? Still, can you relate to a pain so deep that it doesn't hurt anymore? It could be that you've tried giving up on life severally, but only wish this dream comes true when you discover that you're still alive!

I've been at this pain threshold before, too, where I wanted to die. I thought dying could have been better than living then. And I edged gingerly toward the door of suicide. My first suicidal bout came when I tried to control the things, I had no control over. I saw myself as a failure in the very thing that sparked my interest—basketball. I could no longer prove what my grandfather boasted about. I couldn't play on the high school team because of my poor grades, yet I was the manager of my team.

It was most humiliating to cascade down from a winning streak to a string of failures! I plummeted from years of hitting game winners and being the big man on campus, to being reduced to cleaning basket-balls, washing uniforms, filling water bottles for my peers, sweeping the gym floors, and looking at the disgust on my grandfather's face. I'd never forgotten the lines of disgust that mapped his disappointed face after I came clean with him. He dreamed about watching his grandson shine on a bigger stage, which he didn't attain. I had missed my ultimate school job, and I couldn't escape feeling like crap.

Surprisingly, my grandfather swallowed the bitter pill of my reality and advised me to be a good manager. I believed it was his way of consoling me. And for those few ticks of time he spoke, it worked on me pretty well, but not after that. I had other ideas. I was determined to turn over a new leaf by being a good student, make my grades, and join the team next year!

However, life got rough as I experienced several panic attacks. Additionally, I began to indulge in drinking alcohol. It was easy to come by, and I thought it did well clearing off my mind of my problems. Yet, I got stuck in between a wall and a hard place when thinking about how I'd get by with being drunk and attending classes. Since it was mere thought, I retained it like that.

As basketball season progressed, my managerial duties proceeded. I watched the game from the sidelines and bit my fingers as I made a resolve never to put myself in this situation again. *Everything was going to' change*, I assured myself. But my reality opposed my scores to have a better life. I didn't enjoy riding the bus with the older guys; they were harsh and often picked on me for being a manager. Looking back now, I believe it was their way of saying, "You have talent. Get yourself together!" It was a different ball game while I lived in the frustrating moments. For an insecure and fragile teenager, it hurt me to the core, and I quitted being a manager. Pep never asked me why I wasn't a manager anymore when we attended games together. And I played along, never once volunteering my answers.

Horrible and hurtful memories haunt me each time Pep and I visited the hospital before we proceeded to any of the basketball games. My only memorial of that same hospital was horrific. It was the same hospital, my cousin, Kisha, died. I got nervous as I approached the building. We pulled over at the garage, but I never motioned to go in with him. Grandpa came here for a constant check-up. Soon, he taught me how to drive, and I became his designated driver at the expense of driving without a license. Even though he asked me to keep our visit to the hospital secret, I broke this rule. I couldn't bear to watch his strong body become weaker and weaker by the day. I had to say something to someone. That was the actual time I discovered that he'd took those brief visits for his chemo.

Being a private man, he acted out all strong, denying us the opportunity to think of him otherwise. While I pen down this experience, I suddenly recognize the awful similarities between grandpa's concealment of his cancer and my life's conditioning. I realized how much I hid my weakness while my cancerous behavior was withering me away.

Once the secret got out, cancer took its toll on him. He had no reason to be strong anymore. And within the swerving summer period of the 9th-grade year toward 10th grade, cancer claimed my hero's life in the same hospital where my cousin died.

As if his death launched me into an unexpected paradigm shift, I suddenly awoke from what seemed like a dream. I took on my default mode of lashing out questions at God and man. The pain from the wreckage of the first death I experienced, resurfaced. It was at that point that I vowed never to love again because I thought God took everyone, I loved from me. My heart and emotions became calloused, and I was no longer in touch with my feelings. I was a wounded lion who didn't let anyone in my life. In the world of my feelings, I lived detached from everyone around me to protect myself.

In addition to this heart-breaking, debilitating phase of my life, another disaster struck. A day after my grandfather's burial, we received a phone call that a cousin of mine with whom I shared a birthday party with every year, drowned in a nearby lake. As my mom and sibling drove to the lake, I can remember thinking that I wanted to die. This was the second time I thought to end my life. *If living life was this painful, God, please let me die. You have control over this, why do you keep allowing this to happen?* I lamented. We approached the lake, beyond my wildest dream, it was real. I watched my uncle frantically dive down and back up a million times in search of his dear son. He continued to look for him until he was overwhelmed by exhaustion. He had to be restrained to stop. He had the look of despair that I'll never forget. I asked, *"How can this be? We just talked last night about not going to this swimming hole and how we were going to represent grandad."* I was still frozen from the two deaths earlier recorded in my life. I wanted no pact with pain anymore. This not right nor fair. Please don't wake me up!

14

DUCK IN THE WATER

At this point in my life, I already had a front-row seat to a ton of heart-wrenching, toxic, and downright life-altering moments. I was used to being hurt and disappointed that I developed a thick skin for misery. I'd been the main character in some of these tragic moments, although I was in the background. The weight of influence these chains of events have had on my life has been monumental. They have produced stress, abuse, trauma, fear, manipulation, lies, confusion, and in many ways, the blueprint to this book.

Although I know I'm not the only person in the world, or better yet, in my circle, who has gone through so many traumatic situations; I can confidently say that I'm the only one who can articulate and detail my experiences and the numerous effects it had on my life. My experiences didn't just have an impact on an aspect of my life, it had its firm grip on all ramifications and aspects of my aspirations.

If you're reading this, I'm sure you can relate to some parts of my bitter past. Through the exercise of detailing my unscrupulous experiences along life's way, I'm taking back the power from those things that have controlled my life for a long time. Let's take a closer look at things that caused my life to go berserk, and some of the behaviors that each specific traumatic experience caused. I'll also highlight ways that I was able to pull through and heal from my grievous past.

If you're dealing with any of these issues, I'd like to know that you're not alone. I went through the scary stages in my life too. I'd like to show you some specific things that I did to stop the hemorrhaging in my life! Let's go deeper.

First, you must understand, that, to deal with any self-sabotaging behavior, you must be willing to face it head-on. Note that, if you bring forth what's within you, you will quickly begin the process of healing. But if you decide to hide and live in denial, you may end up being destroyed. Now, back to what I did—I made a list of my traumatic experiences, which held me captive for an exceptionally long time and were often regulated. Understand that when you don't know how to deal with overwhelming situations, then you may be helpless when you finally get caught up. You may end up swinging into bitterness, and soon lose yourself.

Here are some of those things that ate me up, both on the inside and outside:

A. **Death**- On many occasions, I have had to witness people being shot and killed in my neighborhood. I saw the internal parts of someone who was shot, scattered in front of me. It was quite unfortunate that he was my mom's friend, whom my brother and I knew very well. He was close to my family, and we maintained a beautiful relationship. When the incident happened, I tried to protect my brother from seeing it, but my body felt as if there was no circulation. I became numb.

Fortunately, the gunshot victim lived, but a part of me died when I took in the scene because I used to imagine such could only happen in a war. It was such a gory sight! The unfortunate event kept replaying from time to time, and I couldn't wipe off the memory.

At another time, my brother and I also witnessed shoot-outs, with bullets breezing past us. That's scary, isn't it? But we had a shield—a large glass window kept us from the bullets flying up in the air. We saw the fire and heard the bullets hit the concrete of the building we stood in. The scent of gunpowder-filled the air that hovered beneath my nostrils, while the fear of death filled my heart. It appears life had splashed before my eyes, and I was not going to survive it.

I won't forget the day we drove to an accident scene in our neighborhood, where the victim was reported dead later that night. While going to bed, the gruesome sight played over and over until I began to have visual and auditory hallucinations. I couldn't sleep because of the images that I witnessed a few hours earlier which shoved my solitude out of the way. I encountered several ugly and terrific sights, and I wasn't even up to fifteen. It was abnormal for an adolescent like me to see those kinds of things and still be sane. I felt reluctant to talk about this, and it wasn't good for me because I couldn't break out of the effect it had on me. Now, it's important to know that, in "uncoiling your corkscrew," you must speak about issues that have coiled your life, even at the expense of losing others. Don't bottle up and mask yourself while dying in silence!

Riding with my dad in his car around the neighborhood was such a joy that I never wanted the spree to end. Even though I wasn't talking to or doing anything with him, it was a rare opportunity, if not one and only, to gallop the city together. The joy of just having him around was simply fulfilling! However, it was short-lived as we approached a stop sign that marked a terminal to my built-up ecstasy. I was surprised when from the shadows, a guy approached my dad's window and pointed a gun to his head, asking for his money. My dad replied, "*I don't owe you anything.*" Somehow, I knew at this point that he was involved in what I would term an "illegal activity." I felt it so strongly that there was more to it than what it seemed, and I could sense danger lurking around us.

I heard my dad telling him, "*allow my son to go out, and we'll handle it*" the gunman quickly conceded. His words were a pointer to the potency of my suspicion. I got out of the car as my dad instructed and walked away. As I began to mooch down the highway, I became scared, nervous, and confused about what was going to happen to my dad. I was caught in the middle of grievous ambivalence; I kept pondering on what the fate of my father would be. I thought, "*Would he survive?*" "*What if he gets killed?*" I was absorbed in my feelings! And the worst of it all is that I couldn't talk about it. We knew catastrophe prowled around, but the next day, we were expected to go on as if nothing happened. I often wanted to talk about it but bringing it up seemed like a taboo. The death of silence!

B. Pornography- While growing up, I remember that those who watched Benny Hill were seen as perverts. First of all, we weren't allowed to watch it at home, so I couldn't access it. Most people who had a sneak peek of it had to pretend they didn't see it. That sounds a little absurd, right based on today's sex inundated society. But that was the behavior of most families in my community. A few friends in school had exposed me to porn videos to spur me to have sex. Soon, I got on board and started sneaking out to watch the dirty videos. It was only then I realized that I drifted into dark, treacherous places.

When I started, I couldn't deal with it. But before I knew it, I went past viewing it on TV screens to walking in the act. I continued to replay the ugly videos and repeat the corrupt acts. I pretended that whatever was happening wasn't real. No one knew about it, and I kept it all to myself.

I'd earlier mentioned a story about me running from a girl who came over to my house just for sex. Well, the backdrop to my running was that I had a skewed vision of sex then. I didn't want it because each time I had no control over acts against my will, I would end up being dispirited and stung. So, instead of having that blah experience, I did myself a favor by running. However, until now, no one knew why I ran or ever asked, and I refused to disclose my reasons. The truth was, deep down in my heart, I had tainted pornographic memories which I had practiced. And I was frightened by the thought of it happening again. I didn't' want the memory to repeat itself.

As I grew older, I struggled more with pornography. Porn is a vicious cycle that will choke the absolute life out of you. The danger and the entanglement of pornography roots deeper than the way it appears across the Screen. There is a stigma it leaves on you, and it paints a permanent picture in your mind, which will influence the lens through which you view women. We live in a generation that has not only accepted immorality but also promotes pornography. According to research, pornography can harm the mind, body, and soul. Below is a list of the aftermath of porn.

- **No sexual satisfaction**- The more you watch porn, the more you become sexually active and addicted to sex. And the less sexual satisfaction you obtain. Also, you will be out for just sex and no intimacy. When this happens, sex loses its essence and the purpose for which it was designed pleasure and reproduction. Aside from that, as a man, you will see women as sex-tools rather than *queens*, which they really are! Some women have lowered their standards and are seeking men just to have it off, and it's not supposed to be so! Another effect of porn is to create a sense of loneliness.

- **Loneliness**- A recent research on porn suggests a close and painful relationship between porn and loneliness for most of its users. Each incremental increase in the use of pornography predicted significant solitude. This represents an entrapment caused by addiction. Another study shows that pornography use is associated with relationship distress, disrupted attachment, and a strain on couple bonding. Harm to relationships is due to pornography "sexual script" consisting of eroticism, objectification, and promiscuity. Although staged film provides temporary relief, it ultimately induces greater feelings of loneliness and isolation, disrupting normal attachment behavior, which often leads to greater difficulty when it comes to forming stable and satisfying relationships. This further increases the likelihood of using pornography as a substitute for intimacy, at least in my case.

- **Porn encourages isolation**- Do you know that isolation is called *"the porn addict's worst enemy?"* Porn makes you withdraw from people; it demands isolation. In truth, anything you do in secrecy usually leads to shame. When you're isolated, you open your mind for the devil to play with, then you begin to dive deeper into pornography. And because you're not proud of it, you want to hide and explore the moment. It is expedient to understand that you can't share true intimacy with others from a shameful place. More so, it will be difficult to grow and mature as a person and to reach our full potential as people.

I wouldn't claim to be a porn expert, but it had it grip on me in the long term. And, I can say without a doubt that the grip of pornography is deadly. It kills dreams, relationships, and you as a person. I thoroughly advise that you seek help if you're engulfed in this addiction. Don't allow shame and pride to restrain you from reaching out for help. You can overcome it just as I did.

C. **Alcoholism and drugs** - As a young boy in my teenage, I watched people smoke Crack, do lines of cocaine, and drink an insane amount of alcohol, regularly. This was the norm, so I didn't think of it as alien. Countless times, I observed fights, shootings, chaos, and sexual favors because it was the culture of my neighborhood. The funny thing is, it never dawned on me that this was strange or abusive. So, I was comfortable with the everyday-life I grew up in.

Likewise, the word *"addict"* wasn't tossed around unless someone smoked Crack. Due to my early exposure, I knew of crackheads who were addicts, whom I respected and cared for immensely. I can vividly recall taking the trash out on one of the nights and seeing a group of crackheads surrounding the garbage for food. My heart was broken as I watched them from a distance because I knew those people. Yet, I couldn't recognize them when I saw them wallow in their addiction, around the rat-infested and toxic garbage. Smoking crack seemed like the only thing frowned at when it had to do with drugs in my neighborhood, although nobody openly spoke about it. Some people would mildly say, "Don't smoke Crack." However, some drugs appeared *"socially accepted."*

So, it was easy to get acquainted with the stench of alcohol because I grew up around it. It was all-encompassing, from family functions to local ball games, and we had many beer stores in my neighborhood. Inasmuch, on Martin Luther King, where I was raised, there was a store directly across the street, and a pool hall was probably 1000 feet away from our apartment. I could always hear the music glaring at night, fights that would break out, and a host of other things. There was rarely a calm moment in my neighborhood because of the lifestyle of its society.

It was quite unfortunate that I had to witness my dad struggle on Crack. And this strained our relationship. I detached from him because I couldn't bear the shame of introducing him to people as my father. In as much as I was a little, it wasn't too hard to figure out what I was trying to hide.

The height of it was that my mom also struggled with alcohol. Almost every weekend, she would go out, drink, get drunk, and fall under the influence of alcohol. I wasn't strong enough for her weight, so I couldn't always carry her. I often would call someone strong to come across town and pick her up, and I'd make sure she's safe. Sometimes, I would pull over for her to vomit, as I drove her home. Then, on getting home, I would clean her up, make sure she drank water, and get her in the bed safely. Other times, she'd prefer to stay on the couch.

I couldn't always sleep each time she was this way because I felt it was my responsibility to make sure she didn't choke on her vomit and die. So, I was usually terrified to fall asleep. However, she always made it through the nights. Then, subsequently, she'd try to get over a hangover. Now, I still couldn't talk about it because I knew it would make her embarrassed. I also kept it secret from my brother so that it wouldn't affect him. This was my life a juggling act, on a secret stage.

D. **Abuse**- when I was about 13, I watched men fight their women in public, and I often felt powerless because I always wanted to stop them and help the women. But I knew I couldn't interfere. However, everything changed the day I witnessed my dad fight my mom near my grandmother's yard. I could hear my mother scream in pain. And all I was able to do was, run into the house, grab one of my trophies, and ran toward where the scream came from.

I took a swing as hard as I could with the intent to harm my dad. I can't remember if I hit him, but I do remember hating him because of his thoughtless actions. I developed such deep hate at that moment, and I can remember the rage I felt toward him. Maybe I would have shot him right there if I had a gun. After the episode, we got back to my grandmother's apartment to sleep. But I was so shocked that I couldn't sleep, and my shock absorber refused to function at that point. I was so hurt! So, hurt because I had seen the terror on my mom's face. I had a lot of other sad experiences, and that contributed to the way I felt and the kind of thoughts that were coming. I realized that I kept being angry. I now know it was rage because the thoughts I had were not normal. Another untreated underlying issue. Let's press forward. I hope this is spurring some memories that you need to be healed from.

E. **Lies and Manipulation** – Lying is easy until you are caught in the act. And it becomes part of you when you have a ton of practice at it. How do you react when a Jehovah's Witness knocks on your door on a Saturday morning? What do you tell them? Don't you tell them that you're busy, even when you're not in the least bit? Or you look for another lie, just to send them away. I call it the "hide-at-home lie."

How about bribery? Sadly, you have this happening in the church too. Some leaders flirt or even kiss a woman who's not their wife. When he notices that you might have a nudge of his atrocities, he'll try to keep you shut by offering you some amount. Or probably, he pleads that you don't tell it to anybody. I was in that situation where I had to choose between doing what's right or wrong. Unfortunately, I usually did the latter, because of the pressure of whom I was supposed to protect. This constituted my view of the world, and it had a deteriorating effect on me. I became accustomed to lying, much to my detriment.

It didn't end just yet. I witnessed women caught cheating on their significant other. Marriages failed because spouses weren't committed to their vows. Now, regrettably, the only marriage I thought was stable and successful, the husband ended up leaving his wife for another woman. This also contributed to how I saw life. It looked as though marriages didn't work at all. However, I'm sure that with their questionable behaviors, they indirectly influenced other believers like myself. Of course, if you set fire and allow the blaze to go out of control, it'll burn down everything else around it. This was my case. My environment influenced me, and it affected every part of my life. However, I no longer use this as an excuse, it was my reality not my destiny. Pull your upbringing apart and understand what lurks in you from your toxic environment. It's up to you to confront and Iron out those issues. Deal with them.

15
LIKE A DUCK

If you have ever watched a duck explore the lake or the pond, you might have a view that it's always smooth, graceful, and effortless. At least, that's how it seems viewing from the pond's bank. But if you got close enough to the edge of the water, and there's any visibility through the water, you'll witness just how violently the duck's feet are kicking to maintain his flawless water glide. In my opinion, we might have become like the character of a duck in various aspects of life.

You might pretend that all is well at home, in your relationships, in church, on your job, and quite frankly, with yourself. Or you may show up with your best face on while trying to glide through turbulent storms. I mean ravaging storms that include abandonment, abuse, anxiety, abusive relationships, alcoholism, betrayal, depression, fear, suicidal thoughts, neglect, or poverty. Probably you're struggling to maintain your smooth demeanor amid turbulent waters. Do you feel you've reached your breaking point and don't know which way to turn?

Life seems a million times too painful, and it could give you shrills of wanting to end it.

Don't give up!

Here's my simple advice for you despite all that's working you up. I'd like for you to work on yourself and unleash the greatness that lies within you! You can't change what's happened in your past, but you can decide to make the most of whatever had happened to you. Allow your mind to have a significant shift from your past. In Romans 7:15, Apostle Paul talks about the nature-struggle and decisions that you can't influence. He says, *"For I do not understand what I am doing, because I do not practice what I want to do, but I do what I hate."*

All that you and I have been exposed to has programmed us to operate on autopilot. And sometimes, we don't have to think about what we're doing to fall in line with the program in our head, it just aligns. However, we have to experience a mental transformation. As we dig a little deeper into *Uncoiling My Corkscrew*, I will lead you into a different mindset on your situation, and I'll show you how I uncoiled those things that weighed me down. *Just track with me!*

IV
THE POWER OF
THE CORKSCREW

A shape of its own...

16

THE GRIP OF
SELF-MEDICATING

Sex

Some of the things I ran from in my past were things I knew derailed the trajectory of people's lives. But, at a point in my life, I began running toward and embracing some of them. Now, one of the things I embraced was sex. I did not only want it, but I also passionately craved it with all my being.

So, I asked myself, what changed with me? *"Has the peer pressure of the fantasy of sex got to me?" "Or has the constant reel of the sex tape that I watched over and again lead me here to practice what I saw?" "Did the internal pain cause me to seek sex as a release valve?"* I don't completely know, and truthfully, I didn't care about anything but having my first acceptable sexual encounter.

This was the period of my 9th-grade summer, and I was scared, lost, and confused. I believe I believe my thoughts followed this pattern because I felt it was okay for a young man at sixteen to think that way. I was bent on having one thing—satisfaction. The truth is, then, I didn't realize there was a problem brewing. In retrospect, I see that 16-year-old me: my virginity is gone, and my dream of having sexual intercourse with my wife alone is never to be fulfilled. Now, I think, *What is sacred about sex now?*

Well, what would I say to this promising boy? I'd tell him that sex is more than the euphoria. If done outside marriage, it exhausts one spiritually, physically, emotionally, and even mentally. It won't satisfy you because you're not content with yourself. So, if you're hurt, lost, and confused, having sex won't help you feel better about yourself. The more you engage in sexual intercourse, the more you hurt, because the pain-relief that you identify as sex only soothes the outer you at the moment. The more you relieve yourself, the farther you are detached from yourself, and you'll keep wallowing in pain which may affect others as well.

In truth, sex is not the answer to your wounded spirit. You may have an itch that sex will never scratch. And this could be the traumatizing experiences you've had. Trying to ask someone else to make your pain go away only leads you to a deeper hole with more hurt, because your partner doesn't understand you. And the roller-coaster you're on will still carry on.

When you punch the ticket for sex, and you have so much trauma in your life, whether the trauma is physical, sexual, or emotional, the impact will show up in a host of relational and personal issues. Sex is not the answer. This is a sure way of deepening the coils that are controlling your life. Here is a list of things that I thought would help after having sex, but they didn't.

- *Trying to wash off what happened in the shower.*

- *Vomiting because of the disgust you feel.*

- *Not wanting to be touched by that person after.*

- *Buying sex because it's just sex.*

- *No feelings at all, and you feel forced to please a partner.*

Although this is in no way an exhaustive list because other underlying issues may be going on. Just like in my case, I would drink to have sex, so I'd be out of my mind. But these things don't solve any problems; rather they build up stacks of problems for you and the unwanted wounded sex partner you have. Get a grip, don't let it rip. You need to heal, before you deal with anyone else.

B. Alcohol

It was normal to drink because it was generally accepted. Plus, it was always accessible. So, as a 16-year old, I could buy it in some stores. But just because society sees things as normal doesn't mean the effect on you won't be detrimental. However, in my case, it was fun because my friends and I didn't hurt anyone when we drank. But did we understand the adverse effect? No!

We were just kids having fun with no idea of the long term effects a little fun would have on us. It didn't matter at that time anyway because as long as we could escape reality for a little while, we didn't see any danger or harm. So, I could ignore the voices in my head and move on with life. On many occasions, I drank at parties, after games, and at friends' and cousins' houses. I was already addicted to drinking that I could not walk past it whenever and wherever I saw it. I have realized that when we see others being addicted to a substance, we make them our barometer. In truth, whenever you compare yourself to someone else, it becomes a slippery slope because you may slip and fall in the course of trying to be like them.

So, here in creeps' justification, I could easily justify why I drank. Most notably, I drank to feel good. I do understand at this point in my life, there were other things underneath the surface, pushing me toward some type of relief, or should I say medication. However, there is a question we all must ask ourselves, and it demands a sincere answer. The question is, *"Why do I do what I do?"* Now, know that it's never because you like doing it. There is an underlying reason you may be afraid to admit. For me, my reasons for drinking were:

- Early trauma exposure

- PTSD (post-traumatic stress disorder)

- Anxiety

- Nightmares

- Abuse

- The sudden loss of a loved one

- Panic attacks

Although this is not a thorough list, I hope you can relate and find an alternative option to self-soothe, instead of alcohol.

At some point, I got aggressive. I started noticing my aggression when I drank, and there were no people who wanted to drink with me. On the other hand, it was ok because I wanted to drink alone. Sometimes, I would get into arguments and scuffles with people, especially one of my cousins, and most of the time, it would end in a fight. The main reason was, we were both inebriated, and the only rationale we could muster up out of our anger was to fight.

Unfortunately, one day, I got arrested because of drinking. And, a bystander said, *"I put on a show,"* which means that I fought the cops, called them weak, and wouldn't allow them to put the handcuffs on and detain me. I justified the reason for my arrest. Even though I was wrong, I told myself I was targeted. This behavior in no way alarmed me that my drinking was a problem. Again, I didn't drink every day. But, when I did, I was a loose cannon. I can recall falling asleep behind the wheel in abandoned places because the ability to drive became too challenging.

Now, there was a particular incident that should have made me stop drinking. But rather, it made things worse. I attended a social afterparty that my late aunt (Barbara) hosted for my friends and me. It made me and a lot of friends safe and kept us from being out and possibly driving intoxicated. It was a great plan and a great party as well. At that time, I was with the love of my life. So, everything was going well. However, I got drunk as time went by, and I began to lose consciousness of myself.

When my aunt saw my irrational behavior, she walked up to me and said, *"Sir Smooth, you've had enough to drink, give me your keys and relax."* In other words, you're sozzled to mount the steering. I told her, *"Auntie, I'm fine."* But that was a lie. A short while later, I tried to sneak away to the car with my girlfriend, but my aunt caught me and said, *"Sir Smooth, please don't go, stay here."* Again, I answered, *"I'm fine, auntie; don't worry, I got this."* I became too comfortable with driving under the influence of alcohol, and the courage from the liquor made me think I was invincible and strong enough to drive.

She begged me to stay, and I told her I'd call her when I got to my destination. I left with my lover, hoping that I was in control. We were fine as we traveled, talking, laughing, and enjoying the moment. The drive was about 45-55 minutes down the long dark lonely roads. Suddenly, she fell asleep, assuming that her life was in safe hands because I was on the wheel. Yes, all of that was true until I fell asleep on her life and mine while speeding down the deserted obscure lane.

Not long after I dozed off, the car veered off the road and dangled on the embankment of the canal. So, I woke up terrified. In the middle of that fright, I yelled because I couldn't get the car back on the road. I could see the splash of water, and I can still envisage it as I pen this book. But thank God, I made it out alive. If not, I'd not be writing this.

I was afraid, but I told myself, *I can't die here.* Amidst my fear, I reached to open my door, the water overtook it, and it was impossible to open. As I mustered all my strength to open it and fight against the elements pushing against us, my girlfriend became frightened. So, I tried all I could to calm her and make sure she didn't die at my hands. I crawled out of my seat, feeling the waters up at our knees. Then, I said to her, *"Relax, we're going to get out of here."* I frantically reached over to open the door on her side, and nothing happened.

I proceeded to try again, yet nothing happened. I don't remember if I screamed, *"God help us,"* or I said it in my mind. But I do know I asked for the only help I knew would get us out of that situation in no time. And, that help would come from Him alone. We had no time for questions on how we got there or what did you do. All we needed was immediate help because the car was sinking extremely fast. I kept looking at my girlfriend's face as I held onto her. I was afraid that if I didn't open the car, we would be done for.

Time slowed down, and as I reached for the door to give it all I got; the door flew open with water rushing in. Then we jumped out. She was scared and said she couldn't swim, so I told her, *"I got you; let's go."* She trusted me and got out of the sinking car. We swam to the steep embankment that minutes ago we had driven from. I swam out and positioned myself to pull her up, which I successfully did.

As soon as we reached the road and looked into the water, all we saw was the reflection of the headlights in that dark, deep, murky canal. We made it out, but I broke down emotionally because I believe I knew we had just escaped death. It was 2:30 in the morning and walking down this road was a death walk. As I tried to put myself together, she broke down in tears. I believe she realized what happened. Then, she asked, "where are we going from here?" this question struck me. I looked up and saw a faint light in the direction where we were headed, and I told her we were walking to the light.

We started our journey, frightened. I was barefooted because I had to give my shoes to her. At some point, we didn't know where we were; we were lost and confused. But, thankfully, we were alive. As we walked down, it seemed like we were taking forever to get to the light. The light was a pointer to hope, and where we could get another cab to our destination. But I began to lose hope as the only car we saw in the last 40 minutes drove right past us. We heard the voices of animals from the thick, dense forest, and I had my doubts about making it.

I could also hear a faint noise in the distance behind. And as I turned around to see what it was, there were headlights headed in our direction. As the lights got closer, I realized it was a truck. So, as it kept approaching, I waved both hands desperately in a way that showed distress. Sadly, this was our last hope for survival. The truck passed us by and began to hit the brake; then it came to a complete stop. We ran toward with all the strength we had, only to get there and realize that it, the nightmare of losing life was put on hold to the Mercy of God. Frustration ran across our faces, and I broke down into a deep cry. When I realized that my mistake of not listening to my aunt's wisdom didn't cost us our lives, I was overwhelmed and overjoyed with emotions. All I could say was thank you, Jesus.

The gripping pain of deciding the influence of alcohol almost cost our lives. Not just my life and hers, but that of our kids. I would have killed my dreams, and this book wouldn't have been written. Now, selfishness could be dangerous. It doesn't only affect your life but affects everything connected to you. So, before you think of acting selfishly, think of the possible consequences. You may not be an alcoholic, but the decisions you make while under the influence of something can be devastating. I could tell you how I lost my basketball scholarship, plus many relationships, and promises that I couldn't live up to because of drinking.

Do stories like this sound familiar? If so, you need help. And, you will have to admit that you're powerless over alcohol and every other substance. Reliance on your strength equals failure. There should only be one source that's controlling your life, and that's the power and Spirit of God. You can call it energy, source, or whatever you want. However, I choose to call it *God*. Whatever you do, nurture this relationship with your source because it's the only force that can drive any negative substance out of your life.

As we proceed, I will still show how alcohol and other things incorporated with alcohol led me deeper into a life of continuous suffering. Another stronghold in my life was weed.

Weed. "You start your journey into outer space, you see yourself in the light, and you're still feeling out of place. So you are standing in the tunnel of eternal light, and you see the ones you never learn to love in life, make a choice, let it go, but you can back it up; if you ain't at peace with God, you need to patch it up. But if you ready, close your eyes, and we can set it free. There lies a man not scared to die, may he rest in peace." This Scarface verse was the song heard when I saw a man die of weed. And it always popped up in my head each time I smoked weed. Most times, I'd get to the point of being paranoid and completely scared.

One day, my heart seemed like it was beating out of my chest. My breathing accelerated, and my mind was uncontrollable. My walk from the basketball court, which was a 5-minute walk, seemed as if it took 2days. Why? Because I was thinking about the means I'll devise to hide my being high from my parents. How was I going to pretend that I was not going to die? Why is this making me feel this way when it makes everyone else that smoke feel good?

Why me? Why now? Why? When I finally got home, I proceeded to the bathroom and tried to wash the odor and the feeling of being high off my face. I looked into the mirror and saw that my eyes were red. I was scared because I couldn't shake the feeling of death. I thought to myself, *"If I don't tell my mom, she won't know what took me out." "If I tell her, she'll know I smoke weed."* So, I began to walk to her room to alert her of my state. As I approached her door, I was overtaken by something that caused me to begin to preach. I faintly remember trying to stop but to no avail.

I couldn't remember what anybody said or did. All I remembered was riding in the car with my pastor and walking into the church office. I sat down on the couch while he sat in his chair, and we started to talk. Now, this was the beginning of my many couch experiences. He counseled me, told me a lot of great things, and prayed with me. He talked about what was going on with me from a spiritual perspective. This single action boosted my respect for him that night. I was already intrigued by what he did, but that gave me a different perspective. I got home and flushed the rest of the weed I had down the toilet. However, I was still on the hook for about $250 because I was secretly selling weed, and the plot thickened.

The next morning, I continued my routine. I went to school as if nothing happened, but the feeling of the episode left some residual discomfort. I was already uncomfortable in my skin, now the juggling act of hiding the show I put on last night was too much. I didn't tell anyone other than the guy I was indebted to. And, to my surprise, he understood. I wish I could tell you that I never smoked again after that time. But the reverse was the case. To add insult to injury, I had the same experience in front of about five friends. We smoked and walked to the park, and I began to feel my heart palpitating. And, somehow, we got back at my aunt's place. When we got there, I kept repeating to myself, "Please, no, not here, not now."

As we entered my aunt's house where we spent the evening, I walked into the restroom, trying to wash off the feeling and to calm down from being high ultimately. The preaching started again, and this time, it was in front of a bunch of strong full of testosterone male counterparts. However, there was no counseling this time. I remember one of my friends bringing me water. When I got the water, I drank, with my eyes closed, and made peace with all of them, because I felt that I was going to die at that moment. However, the reverse was the case; I didn't die. I woke the next morning, surprised.

That day in school, I expected to breathe my last. I was numb to what was going on, and I felt like I wasn't in my body. Does it sound strange to you? I wouldn't say I knew my reality then. I was ignorant about my entire environment. Now, I had a friend who didn't want to smoke with me. He would often say, "Bro, play ball, and forget about smoking." Great advice! So, to hang around my friends, I knew I had to prove that I could smoke weed without causing everyone to blow there high because they were concerned about me.

I knew that if I continued to drink, it would have to keep my anxiety at a calm, then I could also smoke weed without being worried that the chemicals that would trigger whatever that caused me to spazz out. It was a mixer for me. It amazes me the links we all go through to avoid or ignore how we truly feel, which is completely normal. Now, since I didn't have an alternative self-soothe therapy, I had to stick to the available means to escape my inner turmoil. Although they were detrimental, they were all I had, and I was fine with them.

Isn't it sad that in trying to avoid the feeling of misery, you do things that drive the problem deeper? Imagine bathing in addictive substances, which are, first of all, harmful to your health and only have a momentary solution. So that instead of receiving the help you reached for, you end up hurting yourself the more. Have you found yourself repeating these self-defeating habits, only to discover that your temporary fix only prolongs the pain to the next day, while forcing you to repeat the process all over again? If you don't deal with what's dealing with you, consider yourself dealt with by whatever it is that has a hold on you. Understand that you can't rule over what you're subject to.

So, you don't want to continue the vicious cycle of being a puppet on a string in someone else's play. You're called to be the producer, the actor, one who has a starring role on this stage called earth. It will be a travesty to continue doing cameo appearance to your show while the addiction takes the lead role. It is important to know that you have the power to uncoil your corkscrew as soon as you get serious about being serious with your life.

15
WHAT IS IT?

After I lost my cousin and my granddad, I made a vow to myself that I wouldn't get too close to anyone else. If you've ever lost a loved one, you will know that it hurts too much to part ways with love. I incorporated this into my lifestyle. I had to put barriers around my heart, fence it with iron and keep love out. Each time someone said they loved me; I took it as a grain of salt. Love was twisted to me, and I didn't quite understand how it did hurt so much if it was love. I'd heard all my life that *"God is love."* However, I didn't trust this saying because I felt that love doesn't take; it gives.

Remember that earlier on, I'd mentioned that I didn't know anyone that wasn't cheating on their wife or girlfriend. My worldview was tainted, so I wanted to protect my heart at all costs. I didn't want to be a victim of love. Also, at this point in my life, I knew very well how to manipulate relational situations. To be candid, I was a cheater. A cheater is not just a cheater; such a person is a liar, manipulator, becomes cunning and twisted in thoughts. Their life is not straightforward, so you can't trust them with anything, not even your love. If you're a cheater, life becomes an illusion, and you pull others into the twisted version of your world. At least, that's what I noticed about myself. Now, I will own mine, and the quicker you own yours, the faster you grow from it.

But on the other hand, I knew I needed love, although it was not to the real core of me because I'm a lover. So, I didn't trust someone enough to open the space in my heart at the moment. However, I found a young lady who was intriguing to me. But know who I was, and I felt she was more superior. So, I got intimidated and couldn't woo her. I was afraid that if I tried to pursue her, it would expose more of who I wasn't, and I didn't want to take that risk. I can say that most of the people who are hiding behind their pain are also very prideful. And I happened to be in the most category. So, with my pride, shame hurts, and insecurities, I tucked my tail between my legs and ran like the stray dog, which I was.

I ran into less challenging situations, or better still, non-committal situations that wouldn't call my mess to the surface. Know that this may work for a minute, but it ultimately leaves you empty and settling for things that don't ignite your fire. Now, not opening my heart was a dangerous slippery slope for me. Because as you continue to barricade your heart in, you keep fresh flowing relationships out. I was a superstar at detached non-committal relationships. However, I wanted to be close to someone, but the fear of being hurt and abandoned made it difficult. We often rehearse the pain of our past, which is ultimately detrimental to our future.

The seeds that I planted in the garden of my heart were of no good use to myself, and it was affecting those who fed on my garden. In short, I was a toxic plant that appeared to be good for the soul. Although I wasn't all that bad, I wasn't healthy enough to take the hand off of any innocent young lady, knowing that I wasn't capable of being a great guy. I lied to myself and to others obviously out of selfishness, to pretend to be exactly what someone needed me to be. I even fooled myself at times, believing that I was God's gift to humanity. It sounds arrogant now, but it made sense to me then. Can you relate?

A. Love

Concerning love, I'd say that I was in love with my high school sweetheart back then. Can you remember her? However, based on my skewed sense of what love was, if you haven't guessed already, I didn't know what love was, other than *"God is Love." "I love you, mom," "I love you, grandma," and "I love, you brother."* I loved it because I was supposed to love all those people I mentioned. I didn't treat people bad; I was generous, I wanted everyone to feel comfortable around me, and I didn't pick on people. I didn't feel right about doing those, and it would hurt me if I tried to do them. So, based on that understanding, I was a loving guy. However, what is love in a relationship, or what is love? According to the greatest life Manual ever inspired, the Bible, *"love is patient, love is kind. It does not envy; it does not boast; it is not proud..."* I would like to add that love is not boastful, arrogant, or rude. Love does not insist on its own way; it is not irritable or resentful; love does not rejoice in wrongdoing but rejoices in the truth." Love never ends—It's timeless.

But how was I to love when I lied, cheated, and manipulated until I was exposed. I did these things, and I promised never to do them again. Just after I pledged not to repeat them, I lied again. I tried hard to be a good and faithful young man, but it wasn't in me. I didn't have what it took to take up the task. I wasn't strong enough at that time to fight off the temptation. It is not possible for someone who's hurt, is not open for healing, to love another person. They could be destructive.

If someone says they love you and their actions exhibit negative traits, that's not love. I'd rather call it co-dependency, toxicity, or any other thing other than love.

B. Codependency

Do you rely on people for approval and a sense of identity? Anytime you allow someone's behavior to affect you, and you are obsessed with controlling that person's behavior, you may be tethering with them in the co-dependency zone. However, there's more to it. Tag along as I take you through this interesting phase of my life where I got plagued with being co-dependent. Hopefully, you'll relate to some of the behavioral patterns.

Firstly, I'd like you to bear this in mind as we proceed on this self-unveiling journey that,

- *There's a difference between loving someone and being trapped with someone.*

- *There's also a clear cut-out mark between giving to coax someone into liking you and giving from the heart posture of generosity.*

- *There's a difference between narcissism and self-love.*

- *Finally, there's a difference between self-centeredness and being concerned about yourself.*

Now, because all I knew was losing loved ones to either sickness or something disastrous, I withdrew from people a lot. Why? I didn't want to get attached. I feared being hurt again by their absence. The trend was that if I opened my heart up to someone, I'll cling to them, eventually, even at an alarmingly toxic level of relationship. So, to evade the risk of feeling pain if they left, I'd go the extra mile; I'd do anything—anything! Yes, even if it strained me in the relationship, I didn't care.

This brings to mind a lover I passionately cared for. She got into a sacred and vulnerable place with me and broke through my walls. I was head over heels crazy about this lady that I completely lost control of every preset ambitions of keeping aloof, and never allowing anyone to draw close. Yet, I wasn't good enough for her, but I was good to her. Although she professed her love to me, I realized over and again that she desperately tried to let me go. When I noticed this, fear gripped my heart; I told her not to leave me. I begged, sobbed, and pleaded. I knew she was seeing someone else, and that would help her to get over me quickly.

Truthfully, she was just as toxic as I was. However, she had control over me, and I was willing to be controlled. One evening, I went over to her place. She reluctantly allowed me in and gave me her terms, which was to leave whenever her friend came over to take her out. Of course! Why not? I agreed. All I needed was an opportunity to fit in a little space. So, I had to opt for the option that was somehow favorable to me. While we were together, I watched her get dressed, and I savored her beauty. I thought, *Marvin, you're one sick dude to painfully drool as you watch her get dressed to go spend the evening with another guy.* Would you blame me? I didn't blame me for being so sick either. I deserved that because I caused her the pain by clinging. She wouldn't do this if I did what was good for her.

As we conversed, her phone rang. And, oh, I won't forget the look on her face when she asked me to leave. She gestured that someone was on his way to get her. Although she never loved that she hurt me, she felt she was doing what was best to quench her unbearable pain. I felt like a little child, glowering and helpless. However, I grasped that she tried to pass it across that she was tired and done with me.

I left as agreed. But to make matters worse, I passed the guy on the staircase as I left. He didn't know me, but I was certain he came for *my girl*. I swallowed my pride and felt my heart rent inside of me. As I wobbled out of her apartment, I only hoped she'd notice my reluctance to leave and see the pieces of evidence of my broken heart marked on my disappointed face.

After I gave up the relationship, I discovered that I tried to salvage her from everyone else but myself. My soul was knitted to hers, negatively. I'd do all the irritating stuff like cleaning and laying her to sleep whenever she was high on a nightcap. I couldn't help but wonder, was I in love, or was I a mere caretaker creating situations that needed my assistance to be cared for? In most cases, whether alcohol is involved or not, anyone might portray co-dependency behaviors if you tried walking in my shoes, for five or twenty years.

Now, this behavior didn't end here. I repeated it in several other relationships, where I was the victim trying to hold my partner as my prey. Funny but true, once you realize you're exemplifying co-dependent traits, you are actually codependent.

The good news about this fact is that after you identify and work through this behavior, you move on to become an outstanding person. I'd like to inform you that co-dependency is no disease; it's a behavior to check. Yes, you and I crossed the line when we started doing too much, caring too much, feeling too little, or overly engaging. We forgot where the other person's responsibilities began, and ours stopped.

I think it's high time we started paying attention to ourselves. Once we start caring for ourselves, the deficits from our past transform into assets. It builds up as liberating tools to navigate through our beautiful lives. Trust me, trailing the process, you become better equipped for life's journey.

Make sure you don't cross the line. I'm quite big on sports and I know the dreadful implication of winding up a red flag. It usually signifies that something lesser than good is about to happen. When we cross the line into the co-dependency zone, we're flying a red flag high.

Crossing the line may warrant that we have an ulterior motive for what we do, and this usually hurts when it doesn't pull off.

Personally, co-dependency served as a shield to protect me, especially when I knew that letting go would leave me victimized. But it was up to no good. I had to take a more assured route out of the relationship. I had to begin to let God lead me. Friend, you must be willing to lose out on comfort for a season so you can be better. You must let go and trust in God to control the only thing you have control over— you!

C. Manipulation

People don't mind dangling things in front of you just to obtain something they want from you. If you aren't feeling inwardly secure, you may be persuaded to fall for the illusion that manipulation offers. Manipulators tell lies, and victims believe them. The truth is, at some points, we've all been manipulated directly or indirectly. When you're in a sexual relationship with a man, and he claims he wants to be "just friends," know that your *friendship has benefits* reserved for marriage. Understand that the line has been crossed because sex signifies unreserved commitment. Probably, your friend still operates in the friend zone, you may begin to make non-equitable investments in your relationship since you'd given him your cookies.

You might even find it difficult to speak up. To pull through, you may continue to acquiesce your happiness with the friendship, but secretly, you're hoping for more. And there you have it, a robust slap of manipulation has just hit you! You might feel that sex, money, or any other carrot you have in your bag would change that man's mind toward you or how he sees you. Could I let you in on something? Grab your shock absorber as I enlighten you that the dude is visibly aware of every stunt you're pulling. Still, he chooses to continue to reap up benefits without contributing the least bit of commitment. And, unfortunately, you both will end up manipulating each other. He's not directly telling you he won't give you what you want. He gives you just enough for you to stay right on the merry-go-round.

Another cogent point I want you to know about is that manipulation and control go about hand in hand. Most people try to exploit others to serve their agenda. Pay close attention to the people you encounter because some are incredibly good at what they do. I'm writing this from my wealth of experience because I was very skilled then. I'd turn the tables when confronted about issues, and I'd make you question or feel confused about questioning me for my wrong doings. This, I know, because I've been manipulated, and amid manipulation, I asked myself, "Is this what it feels like to be manipulated?" It's gross, vindictive, and evil.

Manipulation comes in the form of disguise. When we manipulate, we hide our real identities. We're not honest about who we are and what we really want from someone, or what our intentions are. If you continue to manipulate, long enough, you'll lose touch with yourself and reality. You become so busy covering your tracks that you're not aware of what others are doing to you. And in trying not to get caught, you don't see anything else.

I know I've lived in the siege of manipulation for long years, manipulating, and vice versa. When I recognized that that's the deal, my heart suddenly turns off against that person and I inadvertently denounce them as being someone good for me.

Matter of fact, I also feel guilty for walking away. Being a great caregiver, I don't want to leave them in that state. However, when we hit the rock of manipulation, getting hit by the same person and thing repeatedly, we crumble into living in co-dependency. We start to live in self-denial. And we must come to terms with the bitter truth that we've burned the bridge of trust. So, we foster doubt within the relationship.

Yet, when you're healthy on the inside, you're better empowered to weld a fight against manipulations. Because you would have to live under a rock to be unaware that manipulators will cross your path. And that'll happen often. You have to be prepared to win. Always!

I believe that many are locked up in the prison of delusion nowadays. And if you happen to break through the bars, you're well past beyond lucky. It's only by God's grace that I'm still here and standing. Getting down to it, manipulation can be a one-time thing or a way of life.

Many relationships have a foundation of deceit. Sometimes, a partner might not love or want the second party but try to endure through the relationship. if we continue in the process, we could end up losing touch with emotions and become unable to express ourselves. I think I've got this for every woman reading these lines. C'mon lady, you've got this! You must ensure you're a major desire and not just exist as an idea in your partner's mind. At the same time, make sure you desire what desires you and not who doesn't, or else, you might wind up as the manipulator.

V

UNCOILING MY CORKSCREW

16
NO MORE DENIAL

Your corkscrew starts with one person, and that's *YOU!* Yes, a lot has happened in your life that caused much heartache and pain. And I want to let you in on this: you can't keep on drinking poison and expecting the other person to die. You've got to discover for yourself that God has a plan for your life, and he wants to turn your ashes into beauty, pain into joy, and defeat into victory. However, this can only happen if you allow him to be your guiding force.

I have had to weave a web that got out of hand. I'd saddled my life's boat almost independently, without anyone actually dictating for me. Nobody determined where I got to in my life, I called the shots! Back then, I remember meeting a counselor in Rehab who straightened me out. He said, *"Marvin, with all of your brilliant ideas, high IQ scores, and your well put together self, your best thinking still landed you here in Rehab. That hurt; however, I think the best thing to do if I'm ever going to love myself and get better is to sit down here and listen for a change!"* Wow! I thought to myself, that he's exactly right.

If my best thinking had landed me in Rehab, then I reasoned that I needed to listen to whatever this man had to say. I was counseled numerous times before this occasion. But this felt completely different because a few times prior, the thought of committing suicide floated along in my mind. However, I couldn't believe I was entertaining the idea of suicide again. Yet as I sat facing this speaker, I knew I had to change course. So, I intently listened because I wanted to change.

Now, the truth is, it doesn't matter how much information we receive about the way to change our lives; we're not going to change unless we're willing. Or like in my case, where it was the only option stuck in between life and death.

Indeed, the power to change lies within you. It's often said that *"life is 10 percent what happens to us, and 90 percent how we respond to it."* At times, life can be overwhelming, knocking us off our feet. Whether we survive depends on what we do about it. It's a hundred percent better to spring back on your feet than throw in the towel. For you to attain the height of positive change in your life, one of the things you'll have to do is to be transparent, just as I've been sharing my story in this book.

Don't bottle matters up and then explode on the inside. It's emotionally healthier to share your burdens and pains with someone you can trust. Unload all the garbage you have in your head to a therapist, counselor, pastor, or a trusted buddy. You might just be sick because you're hiding more than you can bear. It's okay to clear of guilt by opening up to someone.

It's also important to know that who you are is not about what you did. And you're not a bunch of the twisted things that had happened in your life. The happenings that surround your life don't have to define you. Feeling inferior because of the circumstances that trail your life is a direct influence of the lies you believe about you. And you don't deserve to bend to some unruly lies. Understand that the mistakes you made are long past and God forgave you in the very moment you turned to him for help. So, help yourself by forgiving yourself. Release yourself from what's already been done. You, too, deserve to breathe!

For me, I hid behind mediocrity for so long because I dreaded telling my truth to people. But I knew that to become the greatest version of myself, I needed to be transparent, honest, vulnerable, forgiving, and persistent—I mean, I had to be a brand new me! I had to get *comfortable* with becoming *uncomfortable*. It's a beautiful thing to get delivered from the prison of words people put you in. This book is a testament to what God will do for you if you are determined to come out of the shame of your pain!

Understand that when God called you to liberty, there was an exchange. He gave you beauty for your ashes. Isaiah 61:3 perfectly expresses it,

> *"To bestow on them a crown of beauty instead of ashes, the oil of gladness instead of mourning, and a garment of praise instead of a spirit of despair. They will be called oaks of righteousness, a planting of the LORD for the display of his splendor."*

So, allow God to do for you what you can't do for yourself. The power lies in you to wake up and face what has caused you so much inner turmoil. Can you envisage the bigger and better life which lies ahead of you? In truth, there's life in you waiting to be lived out. There's a potential untapped and trapped within you. And you got to let it out! The books are waiting to be written, songs to be sung, films to be written, and a whole slew of other to-dos.

All you need to do is to muster the discipline needed to focus on your strength and hammer out the gold that lies in it. Not only am I referring to those who feel they've almost made it. I'm also preaching this message to the man in jail, the woman in distress, and the hopeless and helpless kid. I'm talking to that lady that has slept with whosoever and feels worthless. My voice cries out to the young man who has been violated and sees shadows of death around him.

Let me remind you one more time that whatever you've gone through is not who you are. It's what you did and it's past. There's still greatness in you. You came from greatness and I want you to know that I love you. I understand that you feel unworthy and uncared for right now, but I also know there's a battalion out there waiting on you right away. So many people are waiting for you to serve your purpose, so don't quit just yet. Although the past stings like a bee, there's still some blossoming that runs through your veins. Live!

17

UPROOT!

You need to understand that what lies in you is greater than what lies behind you. Mahatma Gandhi rightly said, *"What lies ahead of you and what lies behind you is nothing compared to what lies within you."* The more you understand yourself, the more you realize what stuff you're made of, and what things you should put away. Although you may have learned some things from people, some traits are straight off inherent. You need to work on the good and discard the negative traits. I'd like to demonstrate your responsibility by using a garden to illustrate this point.

- **Cultivating**

The process of cultivation begins with breaking and loosening the soil. This process is dirty and requires a ton of groundwork. Most times, the topsoil is hard and rough and prevents good nutrients from going in deep down. After the top layer is broken and you begin to dig a little deeper, you realize that there is fresh soil underneath.

Cultivating involves a lot of time and effort. It's not always a smooth process. Many rocks, weeds, and old roots have been implanted in the soil and need uprooting. So, what you do is to carefully throw away the trash, else the growth will be stunted. Cultivating also actively interrupts the germination of weed seeds. As weeds are removed, so is the competition for vital nutrients weeded off. Now free from hostile competitors, all nutrients are directed to the plant itself, which enables it to grow strong and healthy.

- **Choose Your Plants**

It's your garden; therefore, you decide what fruits or vegetables you want to grow in it. While you may employ labor to cultivate your ground, or even receive advice on what crops will be successful on your farm, you'll have to decide on the type of crop you want to grow, ultimately. Then you go out and get the plant or seeds you want. This is a critical state as whatever your decision is today will determine your harvest by tomorrow. You reap what you sow. It's that simple.

- **Access Your Soil**

Right before you bury the seeds in the earth, you need to survey the soil. It's a good idea to rake over your soil and make sure that it's free from pebbles, sharp stones, or rocks that may kill your plants. You may have to double-check that dug holes are free from foreign materials. Possibly, you may even need to add more soil to the already to bring in more nutrients. If you want, you can take some soil out of your garden and have it tested, making sure it has the right balance to produce exactly what you're planting. You have the right to take your soil to experts to examine. Your mind needs to be fertile ground!

- **Now, you're ready to plant**

Yay! Your garden is all set. You're ready to plant according to your garden plan. Align the plants in rows, based on similarities. Make sure you have enough space in-between your plants, so it can have room to grow and receive ample sunlight and air. Research on how to plant your type of crop, then dig the hole for each plant based on the research you gathered. That would allow the roots of the plant to sprout beautifully. And ultimately, your plants will grow and yield fruits. Be careful of what you allow in your crop. Make time for yourself and always cultivate and articulate exactly what you want and how you want it. No exceptions!

- **Your Garden is Planted**

You did your work by cultivating the ground and removing the stumps, which would have hindered your plant's growth. And you planted exactly what you wanted in your garden, covered the hole, and watered your seed or plant. Now, it's time to maintain your garden. Choose the right people to nurse your garden.

- **Maintaining the garden**

In keeping your garden, you must keep a close eye on your new immature seedlings. It's because this is the time the roots are taking form. However, as you water your garden, you must be on the lookout for threatening and unwanted roots, because they might endanger the real plant. 'Wheat and tares' look alike, and they grow on the same soil, in the same garden. One is dangerous to the other, and that one is the irrelevant one. You must look for a way to uproot the destructive plant. But due to the weakness of your new plants, you may be very strategic in how you pull the weeds that grow to have a stranglehold on your garden. In some cases, you pull them; in other cases, you allow them to grow together with the good plant.

To avoid pulling off the good plant as you eradicate the bad ones, you may need to be careful in order to salvage your plant. You must watch out for when it's convenient to uproot it without destroying the real plant. That sounds so familiar to me because it's about cultivating and planting things in our minds.

You can't continue to allow weeds of negative people, and rocks of old thoughts to create blocks and keep you stuck in self-defeating habits. Also, you can't keep on having an old garden mindset. This means that your thoughts are habitually related to the past beliefs about yourself that undermine your efforts to move forward. I've realized that it is impossible to create a new future when you're rooted in your past. You must clear the old things out of your mind (garden) before cultivating a new you with a brand-new lifestyle.

Candidly, you can't have a changed attitude when your mind has not been renewed. Paul speaking in Romans 12:2, says, *"Do not conform to the pattern of this world, but be transformed by the renewing of your mind..."* So, it starts from the mind. Get to Work. Formulate a plan to get rid of the old and welcome the new. This requires daily attention. You should be able to decide what you take in and what you nurture in your mind. Discard every negative thought from your mind. This may include music, television shows, friends, associates, family, you name it. Don't allow thorns to thrive where your wheat is planted; uproot and dispose of it. Similarly, this applies to your life. You have to put more precedence on you more than anything else.

18

EMBRACE ALL OF YOU

If every male figure were 6 feet 5inches tall, 220 pounds, with washboard abs, that would only appeal to some women. And, possibly, a selected few would settle for them... On the other hand, if every female was 5'5 with a beautiful figure, without a doubt, I know there are men who would desire something different.

Also, to win the presidential election, you need 51% of the votes, that means 49% of the people didn't vote for you. Maybe, they found something they didn't like about you. Or probably, you didn't appease their appetite. All this, of course, is looking outwardly at others, but in retrospect, pales in comparison.

Many people are not confident in who they are. Hence, the yearn for a better version of themselves. Sometimes, they get to the extent of going under the surgical knife or settle for medicine. However, these things don't do a good job, in helping you embrace you. In my case, it took me a longer time than others to focus. Sometimes, I've had a short attention span and could easily get distracted. I constantly changed activities out of boredom, which included an appetite for a constant change of women. I fought to maintain sitting still, and the constant fidget movement from myself drives others crazy, and in all actuality, I don't recognize I'm doing it.

I was usually restless most of the time, then I discovered that watching a TV show or movie, meant a good nap. As I'd mentioned at the beginning of this book, I was diagnosed with Attention Deficit Disorder (ADD. But I chose to be comfortable with it; I embraced the thorn (ADD), and I don't run from it any longer. This became possible because I had to pay attention to what I was doing and study what I had to deal with. So, It's no longer a surprise to me. I try to pay attention as much as I can and would often laugh if I realized I'm pacing the room for no apparent reason or rubbing my head continually, shaking my legs, and more. You get the picture if you've ever been around someone I just described. I've been told not to allow people to put stigmas on me. So, I practice not listen to naysayers and dream killers.

In the course seeking of solution, I was told that CBD oil would work great for me. And somehow, I really needed to try it. I first contem plated it; then, I decided I didn't want anything that would alter me in that way, although it's a natural substance. So, I prayed about It; I've tried to ignore its very existence, I've been ashamed of it. However, I embraced it, and my alternative to all those suggestions are; I'm chosen for this journey with ADD, and how it can propel me to be a better person and ultimately a better human being for others that deal with the same thing. It's a part of me that keeps me humble, keeps me on my knees, and keeps me prospectively thinking that we're all connected in some unique ways.

Your thorn might not be ADD. What is that thorn that is causing you to sink deeper into a mess because you're ashamed of it? Think about it. It may not be as noticeable to you at first because it's your norm. However, if you seek professional help or listen to those who are close to you, you will find some things out about you that keeps you running to the bar, the sheets of a man/woman, or your nearest drug dealer. Now, one of the greatest things in the world for you to do is to "know thyself." you know yourself when you look in the mirror and stop lying to Yourself. Then, you embrace all your scars by leaving those things which are behind you and showing up at the party as yourself. You will begin to see life transform in unimaginable ways.

Now, did I know I could write a book, start my own YouTube channel, and become a life coach and a world-renowned motivational speaker? Yes! However, I didn't have the stage presence to present myself to the world. You can think of this in another way. I was allowing my gift to take me places my character couldn't go. What I was saying didn't line up-in how I was operating. I almost called this chapter the transparency of honesty. Why? I'm not sure.

I believe you have your thorn to be a constant reminder of our need for God, and for us to continually come clean about who we are. It would be best if you told the truth about yourself. Once you come clean and accept who you are, things will begin to unfold in your life like never before. Things can't remain the same. Your thorn is your ticket, and your honesty is your plane ride to higher heights and places you've never been before. It's new, it's unfamiliar, it's adventurous, and sometimes, it's scary. However, this is what life is about "knowing thyself!"

19

GRAVE CLOTHES OFF!

Most people are still entangled in the web of unforgiveness while they continue singing the tune that *"if you knew what they did, you would never forgive them."* Well, I don't need to understand the brevity of what they did, and I'm not saying you should overlook anyone's wrong. However, I'm saying that you shouldn't be caught up in moments that sap your peace and freedom. Don't allow such moments to become your lifestyle or the meal that you continually serve yourself. Nonetheless, you need to know that freedom is in your mouth, and It's laced with your forgiveness. If you keep holding onto hurts and past pains, you will become bitter, angry, and you may end up emitting bad energy, and people won't stay around you.

Now, if this is you, own it. Don't be afraid to cry your last cry and decide to do something drastic to unleash the cork of unforgiveness in your life. Now's the time to get serious about the Poison that's seeping out of your pores. Whatever it is that was done to you, you need to visit the grave. You need to physically go to where that person (situation) was buried and have a memorial service where you talk honestly and openly about your pain and what was done to you.

Be free to express yourself and say all you need to say. You may want to scream, kick, yell, do whatever you must do to release that which is built up inside of you. Right after your pity party or release party as or any name you give it, make sure you're in control of the narrative. Don't fall back into the unforgiveness trap. Decide that you will take the path of peace and freedom.

So, whenever you feel you've confronted the demon that injected poison into your life, and you've memorialized the situation, forgiven the person, and allowed peace to reign in your heart, you get up and walk out of those grave clothes, leaving them right there. *"Take off the old man, and put on the new man,"* and *let the dead bury the dead.* This is how drastic we must be about uncoiling our corkscrew. Our freedom lies in forgiveness.

If you are gripped with hurt from someone who's still alive, know that you're harming yourself, while the other person is still moving on beautifully. So, choose between forgiving that person from a distance or confronting them. Now, this is where you'll need wisdom, because you need to do the right thing, and do it well. Know which of the two your strength can carry. However, if you must confront the person, I'd advise that you go with someone who is emotionally mature, so they'd know how to handle the situation.

I had to be intentional about forgiving everyone who, in one way or the other, violated me. I devised several means to make sure I forgave everyone. Some of the approaches I used were through letters, phone calls, person to person, individually, crying, sobbing. I had to release them from their injustices, and more importantly, cut the string that had me connected to the situation. Was it a smooth process? No! However, it was something I needed to do, so I did it. And guess what? It was worth it! So, you too must take this rough path, if you must grow, live a happy and free life!

20

NO MORE PUPPET ON A STRING

Now, you've identified your issues! You understand why you struggled with trauma, and you understand the stigma came with mentioning you had issues. You've acknowledged you struggled with porn, cheating, alcohol, or drugs, lying, manipulation, and inferiority complex. You've also realized that ADD, ADHD, OCD, and whatever other 'D' you may be dealing with will not cripple you, but they will remind you that you're special. You've forgiven yourself and have done the daunting task of forgiving others and also known that God will forgive you as well. You've understood that there is no one to blame for what you've been through, and you don't walk with a victim mentality.

You've realized your dreams, and you are pursuing it relentlessly. You've become a better person for yourself and your kids. You no longer accept life as it is because you have taken charge of the direction of your life. You've detached from toxic situations and toxic people, and you tell them they no longer have a role to play in your life. You're fine-tuning your script. You no longer manipulate people, but in every situation, you allow others to choose their destiny, even if it excludes you. You're trustworthy, faithful, honest, and full of integrity. Your character proceeds you wherever you go, and it opens business opportunities for you. You're now transparent without being scared. You look at life with a smile, and you embrace the total of you. Furthermore, you unapologetically live your life.

Congratulations, my friend, because you are an overcomer! You are no longer a slave to the past. No longer a Puppet on a string. You, my friend, are a source of inspiration, beauty, and blessings for the world to see. You are on this journey to continue to uncoil your corkscrew, and you are being commissioned to help others uncoil their corkscrew.

Now, know that you are a masterpiece hand-crafted by God.

Reflections

Looking over my life today, I realize that every circumstance and event was a gate that opened me up to the next phase of life. Everything that happened was meant for my good. My mom and dad were divinely hand-chosen and hand-picked for me, just as I was chosen for them, and they're my heroes. In as much as we experienced challenges, my parents also did a marvelous job with me. We all have a beautiful relationship up till this day. This testifies of how forgiveness and healing butters a dry and cracked bond.

At this point, I'd like to say that Mom, I love you. Dad, I love you. And my kids are a blessing to me. Each time I look at them, I see infinite possibilities. I'm so grateful to be a part of this journey that God has graced me to see and witness. I'm a miracle to myself and a blessing to others. I'm not only surviving; I'm thriving. I am the master of my domain. I am the captain of my ship. I am fearfully and marvelously made. I am built to withstand every storm, every tide, and every raging sea. I am healed. I am delivered. I am strong. I am Marvin Williams. *Who are you?*